Basic Book of Weekend Gardening

Dr W. E. Shewell-Cooper has written more than 60 bestselling books on gardening, beginning with *The Garden* in 1932, and contributes to 40 newspapers and journals. He frequently appears on radio and television, and travels all over the world to lecture and advise. He is best known as the champion of compost growing, an organic gardening method which he first researched at the Thaxted Horticultural College, Essex, where he was Principal for ten years. Evidence of the success of this method can now be seen at Dr Shewell-Cooper's famous experimental gardens at Arkley Manor, Arkley, South Hertfordshire.

Recognition has come from many countries, including France (Commandeur de Mérite Agricole), Austria (Fellow and Doctor of the Vienna Horticultural College) and Italy (Cavaliere al Merito). Dr Shewell-Cooper is Director of the International Horticultural Advisory Bureau, and founder and Hon. Director of the Good Gardeners' Association.

W. E. Shewell-Cooper

MBE, NDH, FLS, FRSL, MRST, Dip Hort. (Wye), DLitt

Basic Book of Weekend Gardening

Pan Books London and Sydney

First published 1977 by Barrie & Jenkins Ltd
This edition published 1979 by Pan Books Ltd,
Cavaye Place, London SW10 9PG
© W. E. Shewell-Cooper 1977
ISBN 0 330 25630 0
Made and printed in Great Britain by
Cox & Wyman Ltd, London, Reading and Fakenham

to my dear cousins
John Shewell-Cooper, MA
late Headmaster of the Caldicott Preparatory School
and
The Rev. Irene M. Shewell-Cooper, BA
late Lecturer in Religious Studies

List of illustrations

Contents

Preface

This is a book for people with limited time, but people who want to make the best of their gardens despite this. My basic aim is to tell the reader what to do and when. If you use it as a kind of diary you won't find that you have left pruning your roses too late, or that you aren't going to have any indoor bulbs at Christmas because you forgot to buy them.

It is a book for people who aren't entirely new to gardening – I assume, for instance, that you will have some idea of what pruning is, and know what is meant by an annual. In a book of this size it would have been impossible to explain and illustrate every term – though the glossary and tables at the back are intended to help out the reader when necessary, and there are many other more specialized books on the various areas of gardening which you can obtain from a bookshop or your public library.

Obviously a gardening writer cannot make categorical statements about which week a certain job has to be tackled. The British weather is far too fickle for that, and there are climatic differences from north to south and east to west which mean that roses may be blooming in one part of the country while elsewhere there is still frost at night. So I ask my readers to use their common sense in planning and adjusting the gardening activities, as I have described them, to suit their own particular conditions.

There are, however, a few rules which are always worth following – especially so for those with little time on their hands. First, buy well – don't get old or unhealthy-looking seeds and plants. You can't afford failures. For the same reason always read the instructions carefully – whether they are on shrubs, or seed packets, or insecticide labels. It pays to spend a little time keeping your tools in good condition – five minutes spent sharpening and oiling shears now may mean half an hour less and no aching wrists when you next have to cut your hedges. Weeding is a job no gardener likes. You may think I am obsessed with sedge-peat mulches, but for the busy weekend gardener in particular they are a godsend, smothering weeds and preventing their seeds from establishing themselves.

I have divided the book into months, taking an average four weekends to each month. Sometimes I have some general points to make – concerning tools and equipment, or garden paths and drives, for instance; then I discuss in turn what to do, during that period, with lawns, flowers, shrubs and hedges, fruit (soft and hard – also nuts), vegetables (including rhubarb, which is used as a fruit) and the greenhouse. Some of the plants mentioned are unusual ones – why not try something new? It would be a challenge, and you would be even more delighted with the results.

I have tried to cover as wide a range as possible, in an attempt to please everybody. Obviously not everyone wants to raise asparagus and canna lilies, many gardeners don't have a greenhouse in which to raise young plants, and the idea of a formal pergola in the small garden of a modern house is laughable. Be selective, read the advice carefully, choose what you want to grow, plan your work in the garden as much as possible in advance, and you will enjoy both your gardening and its results.

I would like to thank Mrs Gweneth Johnson, Dip. Hort. (Swanley), a Council Member of the Good Gardeners Association, for reading through and correcting the script, and Mrs Beryl Lovelock for typing it so patiently.

W. E. Shewell-Cooper

Arkley Manor,
Arkley,
South Herts.

January

January is the month to write to seed firms for their catalogues. Many of them advertise in the Sunday newspapers. Some specialize in flowers, some in vegetables, some in exotic fruit and vegetables, some in shrubs, some in herbs, and so on. You can work out the quantities of flower and vegetable seeds needed if you make a plan of the garden first. Try and order all the seeds you will need for the season at the same time; you will save yourself much time and bother later on.

As a new year's resolution, make up your mind to join a gardening association and then you can get free advice on any gardening subject, perhaps receive a monthly newsletter and buy seeds, tools and manures, etc. at a discount.

First weekend

General   Make a gardening medicine chest and hang it on the wall of your garden shed or garage where it will be easily accessible (but not so low that children can get into it). Put in it the various insecticides and fungicides you will need at short notice during the spring and summer. I suggest liquid derris, pyrethrum-derris dust and liquid, Draza pellets, and maybe garlic cloves to prevent the club root disease.

Renew all damaged or illegible garden labels.

Gravel paths that have become loose may be rolled during a damp period to firm them – roll to make a camber towards the centre. Make new garden paths if necessary, using concrete (*plates 3 and 4*), stone flags or Noelite paving. Renew macadamized paths with Decopath, which can also be used on gravel paths.

Lawns   Trim the edges of the lawn with a sharp pair of hand or electric shears.

Flowers   Prune creepers on fences and walls – in particular ornamental vines, honeysuckles, virginia creepers, and the types of clematis that flower on young wood.

Fruit Complete all the pruning if this has not already been done. The only exception is gooseberries, which should be left until March. Early pruned gooseberries are invariably attacked by birds who eat the buds. Burn all the prunings carefully, and, when the ashes are cold, apply them around the trees. Wood ashes are particularly useful for gooseberries, redcurrants and dessert apples. Where apple and pear trees are making too much growth and are not fruiting, carry out root pruning this week.

Complete the winter tar oil spraying, soaking all the branches thoroughly as well as the trunks. If your fruit trees are growing among vegetables, cover with sacks any plants that might get sprayed by the tar oil and be killed.

Vegetables First, a word of warning – never do any digging or forking if there is snow on the ground.

Lift salsify and scorzonera for clamping. Lift parsnip roots and leave them in a heap to be washed by the rain and sweetened by the frost.

If the weather is dry, hand weed the autumn-sown onions and dutch hoe them lightly between the rows. Treat spring cabbages in a similar manner, but draw the soil up the plants rather than away from them.

Blanch endives for three weeks with upturned boxes or pots. Protect late celery by putting dried straw or bracken over the top. Lift large clumps of three- or four-year-old rhubarb for forcing in the dark in heat. Leave the roots out for a fortnight before bringing them under cover. For a later crop cover plants with upturned boxes or pots where they are growing, and surround with well-rotted compost or old leaves. Treat seakale crowns in a similar manner. Cut the blanched seakale when the stems are 45 cm (18 in).

Greenhouse Buy No-Soil compost and sow solanum, gloxinia, streptocarpus, saintpaulia, acacia, leucocorynes, and begonia semperflorens seeds. If you want very early cucumbers and tomatoes, sow your seeds this weekend.

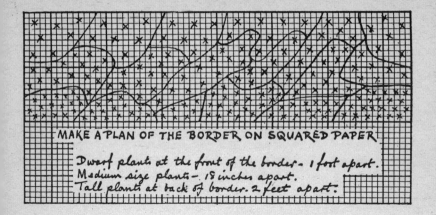

MAKE A PLAN OF THE BORDER ON SQUARED PAPER

Dwarf plants at the front of the border - 1 foot apart.
Medium size plants - 18 inches apart.
Tall plants at back of border. 2 feet apart.

Prune peaches, tying in the fruiting wood. Apply fish manure at 75 g to the square metre (3 oz to the square yard), flooding well. Spray the trees with a 5 per cent solution of a good tar oil wash. Prune vine rods by cutting back the one-year-old side growths to within one bud of their base. Paint the rods afterwards with a 5 per cent solution of tar oil wash.

Take cuttings of late-flowering chrysanthemums. Re-pot pelargoniums, godetias, clarkias and schizanthus, from 7.5-cm (3-in) pots to 14-cm (6-in) ones. Give a top dressing of No-Soil compost to the hippeastrums.

Second weekend
General Use a file to sharpen the edges of tools such as spades and hoes. Clean them thoroughly and then oil them to keep them bright. Repair seed boxes and dip them in preservative.

Flowers Plan and plant a herbaceous border – consult the *Basic Book of the Herbaceous Border*. Plant all kinds of roses firmly, and cover the beds afterwards with medium-grade sedge peat to a depth of 2.5 cm (1 in). Hand weed flag iris borders, and if the bed is not covered with sedge peat, fork between the plants lightly. Tread around the forget-me-nots and wallflowers which you planted in the autumn, since they tend to rise out of the ground after a heavy frost.

Shrubs and hedges Plant deciduous shrubs now.

Fruit Take cuttings of bush fruits. With blackcurrants remove none of the buds, but on gooseberries and redcurrants remove all buds except the top three. See that stakes next to fruit trees are firm and function properly. Use plastic tree-ties which do not rub the trunks; this would let diseases enter.

If you want to grow soft fruits this year, order your bushes straight away and plant immediately.

Vegetables Order seed potatoes for planting in late March or early April. Put them in chitting trays, rose end upwards, in a frostproof room or shed where there is plenty of light. Seed potatoes should be the size of a hen's egg.

Greenhouse Re-pot ferns using plenty of crocks in the bottom of the pots. Prune fuchsias back quite hard. Give the freesias some diluted liquid seaweed fertilizer.

Introduce into the greenhouse, in batches, bulbs growing in pots and bowls. Look over chrysanthemum cuttings to see if damage is being done by leaf-mining maggots; if so, spray with Malathion.

Pot up lily bulbs and put them into a frame or cool greenhouse. Start off tuberous-rooted begonias in a mixture of sedge peat and sand.

Remove the dead foliage of fading flowers from plants in the greenhouse, stir the earth on the tops of the pots to remove moss and, if there are any greenfly about, fumigate the house with any of the modern smoke products which can be bought from chemists or gardening shops.

Third weekend
General Buy in as much No-Soil compost as you will need for the season – it is suitable for almost all plants. Don't stir in the plant foods in the plastic sachet until just before the compost is used.

Flowers Prepare a trench for the sweet peas if the soil is right. Make this a spade's depth and a spade's width; put well-rotted compost into the bottom of the trench at one bucketful to the yard. Fork over lightly the strips of ground required for dahlias and chrysanthemums, adding one good barrowload of compost to 9 square metres (8 square yards).

Where bulbs are starting to come through the soil, fork among them very lightly. If the earth is not sodden out of doors, this is the last possible time to plant daffodils, hyacinths, anemones and tulips.

Make chrysanthemum cuttings. Put cuttings of the late-flowering types in first, and cuttings of the early varieties last. Growths coming up from the base of the old plants must be cut and inserted as cuttings. Choose short-jointed, sturdy cuttings 7.5 cm (3 in) long, and cut just below a leaf joint.

Sow in No-Soil seed compost sweet pea seeds, antirrhinums, dahlias, annual carnations, petunias and hollyhocks.

Fruit Carry out orchard renovation. If a tree is not cropping well it is not worth keeping, and it may be necessary to thin out every other tree. You may feel severe pruning is enough. Follow by applying fish fertilizer or meat and bonemeal at 75 g to the square metre (3 oz to the square yard) all round the trees as far as the branches spread. If you have to make big saw-cuts, clean them up with a sharp knife, and paint them with a thick white lead paint to keep out disease spores.

Obtain fruit catalogues, and place your orders immediately. Some trees of apples and pears will bear three different varieties. These are called 'family' trees and are very useful in a small garden. Cordons are also useful here. They can be planted 60 cm (2 ft) apart, and trained at an angle of 45 degrees on wires. Apple, pear, plum and cherry trees should be planted so that the union of stock and scion is above soil level.

Plant raspberries, redcurrants and blackcurrants. Put straw on the soil 30 cm (1 ft) deep and you won't have to hoe during the following season.

Vegetables Sow a row of round-seeded variety of pea, like Meteor, and a row of hardy broad bean such as Red Epicure. You can only sow if the soil is just right, i.e. not too wet and not too dry. Plant Jerusalem artichokes as you would potatoes, and manure them well; the variety Green Globe is worth trying. Plant rhubarb crowns and shallot bulbs.

Greenhouse Bring a few roots of mint and tarragon into the greenhouse for planting in a mixture of sedge peat and soil. Plant the roots of these two herbs only 1 cm (½ in) deep.

Force strawberries in pots to get fruit in February and March. Plants now growing in 15-cm (6-in) pots out of doors can be brought into the greenhouse to go on shelving near the glass. If you are scrapping an old asparagus bed, bring the roots into the greenhouse and pack them tightly together on a carpeting of sedge peat, on the staging. Put more sedge peat on top, and force the strawberry plants in heat. Keep the peat damp.

Fourth weekend

General The rock garden should be weeded and cleaned now. Heavy winter rains sometimes wash soil away from around the plants, so make up a mixture of loam, sand and peat and top-dress any alpines affected in this way. Work it in among the plants, and don't let any remain on top of the leaves.

Everybody likes making bonfires, but make sure that you only burn woody material, such as prunings (see below), that cannot possibly be rotted down and used as compost. The ashes from the bonfire should be scattered along the rows of gooseberries, redcurrants or raspberries, or, if you don't grow soft fruit, over the rosebeds, or even where the sweet peas and outdoor tomatoes are to be planted this year. This puts organic potash into the soil.

Flowers Order annual flower seeds. Plant a no-work heather garden. Although most heathers like an acid soil, you can now obtain varieties which tolerate alkaline soils. Fork sedge peat into the soil first. Plant heathers 30 cm (1 ft) apart, in drifts of five or six. Cover the soil with sedge peat afterwards to prevent weeds growing.

If you want to grow climbing roses or ramblers, erect a pergola or trellis over which the plants may be trained.

Fruit Fig trees by walls need some protection against frost – hang some old sacks or sacking over the branches. Remove it when all risk of frost is past, in about mid-May. Prune outdoor vines. Cut back the laterals or lengths of one-year-old wood to within one plump bud of their base. Prune peaches and nectarines, tying the fruiting laterals to the wires.

Vegetables If the ground is hard with frost, wheel out well-rotted compost or manure on to the ground where it is to be forked in. If you have already forked in manure, apply a surface dressing of carbonate of lime.

Make up a mushroom bed in a shed, cellar or attic. Buy special mushroom compost and put it into boxes after it has been moistened. Put the spawn in a week or two later.

Greenhouse   Sow batches of mustard and cress, for cutting. To prevent grittiness lay a piece of well-soaked sacking over the soil, and sow the seed on this. Water well. The cress needs sowing three days before the mustard, so that they are both ready together.

For lettuces under glass, sow seeds of the variety Cheshunt Early Giant in boxes, and when the plants are up put them out into the border, about 30 cm (1 ft) apart. For early tomatoes, sow seeds of a variety like Grower's Pride in boxes or pots at a temperature of 19°C (65°F).

Sow the seeds of an early variety of cauliflower in boxes filled with No-Soil compost. When the plants are about 2.5 cm (1 in) high prick them out into pots for further growth.

If you like early vegetables, sow seeds of the French bean Masterpiece in No-Soil potting compost in 15-cm (6-in) pots; sow five seeds round the edge of each pot, 2.5 cm (1 in) deep. Do not water the compost until the seedlings are through. For very early cucumbers, sow seeds in compost in 7.5-cm (3-in) pots, two to a pot, 1 cm ($\frac{1}{2}$ in) deep. Put the pots above the hot water pipes for quick germination – cucumbers love bottom heat.

February

February can be a freezing month and the soil quite hard. On the other hand, in a mild winter it may be possible to cultivate the soil. So please remember that the instructions given for this period may sometimes not be able to be carried out until a fortnight or three weeks later.

First weekend
Lawns   Sweep the lawn clean of worm casts, leaves and stones. On a nice dry day give it a light rolling. If the weather is good enough, patch the lawn with new turves. If the sward is bumpy, lift the turves where there are mounds, take away some of the soil underneath and replace the turves.

Fruit   Continue to prune hard and soft fruit if this is not yet completed. Take more cuttings of redcurrants, blackcurrants and gooseberries, and plant more soft fruits if necessary.

If it wasn't advisable to use Mortegg during December or January, ask the chemist for a DNC wash and spray with this now. Wear gloves and protect your face with a smear of petroleum jelly.

Keep grease bands on apple and pear trees tacky – scrape the banding material with an old comb.

Vegetables   On a warm, sheltered, sunny spot plant out some lettuce seedlings 27 cm (9 in) square; at the end of the garden plant Jerusalem artichoke tubers 45 cm (18 in) apart in drills 10 cm (4 in) deep.

Sow a long pod broad bean – Longfellow is a good variety – 7.5 cm (3 in) deep if the soil is not sticky. Treat the seed first with a pre-emergence dust. Sow the dwarf pea Meteor in drills 5 cm (2 in) deep with the seed 7.5 cm (3 in) apart. Treat the seed just as for beans.

In the south and south-west it may be possible to sow parsnips in drills 1 cm ($\frac{1}{2}$ in) deep; mix radish seeds with the parsnip seeds – this will mark the rows because the radishes show through more quickly than the parsnips, making it easier to hoe.

Greenhouse   On damp sacking sow mustard and cress once every 10 days. To have early melons, sow seeds of the variety Dutch Net (*plate 8*) in 7.5-cm (3-in) plastic pots filled with No-Soil potting compost. Sow lettuce seeds, variety Hilde, in boxes containing firmed compost, and in 7 weeks' time you should have plants for setting out in the open.

Sow seeds of freesias and perpetual-flowering carnations for August flowering. Propagate the begonia Gloria de Lorraine by means of leaf cuttings. Use a sharp sandy compost. Pot up, into 7.5-cm (3-in) compost-filled plastic pots, gloxinias that have started into growth. Pot on cypripedium orchids. If you haven't yet completed the division of the ferns and the potting on, do this now. Pot up the rooted late chrysanthemums into 7.5-cm (3-in) pots.

Second weekend
General   Because the days start to lengthen, plant growth starts to improve. Light always plays an important part in this process and great activity may therefore take place in the greenhouse. Frames and cloches need to be got ready. Root cuttings generally develop well and may now be struck.

Flowers   Give the crown imperials a dressing of well-rotted compost or medium sedge peat all over the area in which they are growing, to a depth of 2.5 cm (1 in). In the south and south-west plant corms of anemones and crowns of lily of the valley.

Prune climbing roses lightly – tie them round and round the posts on which they are trained or space the branches out evenly against the wall.

Shrubs and hedges   Plant hedges like beech – Quick, Blaze, Purple Flash, Green Glow, Slow Pink and Pink Paradise. Apply a fish manure to established hedges at 75 g (3 oz) to the yard run.

Fruit   Cut back the raspberry canes planted the previous autumn to within 15 cm (6 in) of soil level. Protect from birds fruit buds of wall fruits, gooseberries and redcurrants by spraying with a garlic mash. Thin out the spurs on old fruit trees, especially on pears. Consider planting the family fruit trees mentioned earlier. Always plant shallowly, but firmly, stake well using a Rainbow tree-tie.

Cultivate lightly between strawberries, but not if the land is 'sticky'. Varieties of raspberries which are to fruit in the autumn, like New Zealand Lloyd George and Hailshamberry, should be cut down to within 5 cm (2 in) of soil level.

Vegetables Sow summer cabbages and summer cauliflower in a frame. Plant seakale thongs 45 cm (18 in) apart, and sow parsley seed as an edging plant. Sow radishes on a warm south border. Divide clumps of chives and replant 22 cm (9 in) apart – these make good edging plants too. Apply dried blood at 50 g (2 oz) to the yard run to winter spinach and spring cabbage. Hoe lightly afterwards.

Plant thongs of horseradish in special raised beds. In 'early' parts of the country plant early potatoes like Sutton's Foremost, Arran Pilot or Ulster Chieftain in rows 60 cm (2 ft) apart, with tubers 60 cm (2 ft) apart in the rows. Put well rotted compost or medium-grade sedge peat in drills at one bucketful to the yard run.

Greenhouse Pot on young tomatoes, now about 7.5 cm (3 in) high, into 9-cm (3½-in) plastic pots filled with the usual compost. Keep the temperature at about 16°C (60°F).

Give late-flowering cinerarias and primulas diluted seaweed manure as they come into flower. Stake and tie up the late-flowering daffodils and hyacinths. Start the tuberous begonias in heat if this was not done in January. Bring the dahlia tubers into the greenhouse and start them into growth. Bring in the stools of the blue salvias also. Separate the cannas and take cuttings of buddleias.

Look out for greenfly and spray with liquid derris or fumigate in the evening with a suitable smoke. Ventilate the greenhouse carefully – see that there are no cold draughts, but don't let the atmosphere get stuffy.

Third weekend
General If the winter is a hard one, you may well have to do at this time all the jobs you weren't able to do in January or early February. It will pay you to go back through the book and tick them off one by

one. Don't be tempted to start the work for the fourth week of February until all the jobs listed for the first three weeks have been done.

Flowers If you have some wallflowers in a frame under Dutch lights, the plants can now be put out where you want them to flower. You can also plant out polyanthus at the same time. Lift large clumps of montbretias, split them up and replant.

Fork very lightly in between autumn-planted primroses, pansies, and other spring bedding plants. Dig up the corms of gladioli not dug up in the autumn, clean and dry them and replant in a fortnight's time. Sow sweet peas under cloches or Access frames, nick the skins of those with hard coats.

Sow seeds of half-hardy annuals for planting out later. Sow seeds or rock garden plants such as erinus alpinus, papaver alpina and silene alpestris. Prick out the seedlings of the salvias, zinnias, and antirrhinums 2.5 cm (1 in) apart into No-Soil compost in boxes.

Shrubs and hedges Order evergreen flowering shrubs needed for planting later in the spring. Prune the hardy fuchsias, the cornus, rhus, late-flowering spiraeas and deciduous ceanothus. Cut the hypericum calycinum to within 5 cm (2 in) of ground level.

Pruning a wisteria down to two buds

Fruit To prevent peach leaf curl, spray peaches and nectarines with colloidal sulphur just as the buds are starting to move. Protect early-flowering wall fruits with two thicknesses of hessian to prevent frost ruining the blossom.

If a fig tree is making too much growth, dig a semi-circular trench 90 cm (3 ft) away from the main trunk, and cut all the roots you see. Dig down to 90 cm (3 ft). Prune morello cherries, cutting out the old wood and tying in the new. Cut out old wood of blackberries, logan-berries and nectarberries and tie in young growths with trellis or wires.

Prune cobnuts and filberts when you see the catkins starting to open – this helps to distribute the pollen. Cut off suckers growing at the base of the trees. Apply a fish fertilizer all over the soil as far as the branches spread, at 75 g (3 oz) to the square yard. If you haven't got a nut tree and want one, plant it now.

Vegetables Sow celery seed – varieties such as American Green or Greensnap – in boxes of compost in a temperature of 13°C (55°F). Leek seed can be sown in compost in frames; parsley seed may be sown in the same compost in boxes, to raise plants for planting out in a frame or under cloches.

On a sunny, warm border add medium-grade sedge peat at two bucketsful to the square yard, and rake the soil level. Sow seeds of All the Year Round cauliflower and Greyhound cabbage in rows 15 cm (6 in) apart. Apply carbonate of lime to the surface of the soil after-wards, at 125 g (5 oz) to the square yard.

Greenhouse Take geranium cuttings in No-Soil compost, and plant them round the edge of a 15-cm (6-in) pot, 3.5 cm (1½ in) apart. Take cuttings of early-flowering chrysanthemums, begonias and abutilons.

The autumn-struck cuttings of geraniums and pelargoniums can now be potted up into 7.5-cm (3-in) plastic pots. Those already grow-ing well in 7.5-cm (3-in) pots can be potted on into 15-cm (6-in) pots. Delay this as long as possible, however, because of the extra space plants take up in their larger pots in the greenhouse.

Fourth weekend
General Don't waste the long winter evenings, but get hold of some good gardening books and read.

Lawns It may be possible this weekend to give the lawn its first light mowing, and afterwards apply powdery compost at a bucketful to the square yard.

Flowers Plant bulbs such as scillas, ixias, aconites and ranunculus. Give the early-flowering irises a little protection. Plant outside the bulbs that have finished flowering indoors.

Make a pool or water garden. Construct a rock garden for alpine plants.

Give rosebuds a dressing of medium-grade sedge peat 2.5 cm (1 in) deep and some fish fertilizer at 75 g (3 oz) to the square yard. Don't forget to top-dress in a circle around the ramblers and climbers as for ordinary roses.

Shrubs and hedges Look over the flowering shrubs and give the hedge a mulching of sedge peat.

Prune the Jackmanii group of clematis quite hard – remove the weak and unripe shoots completely, and shorten the stronger growths to within 30 cm (12 in) of their base. Prune shrubs such as buddleia, hydrangea and spiraea.

Fruit It is invariably better to grow apples and pears in grass, rather than on cultivated land because the fruit is always better-coloured and better-flavoured. When the trees are four years old, sow grass seed all over the soil at 25 g to the square metre (1 oz to the square yard).

Spring planting of strawberries is never as good as August or September planting, but it is better to plant now than never. Prepare the soil where the strawberries are to go in by lightly working in well-rotted compost or medium-grade sedge peat at two bucketsful to the yard run, and fish manure at 75 g (3 oz) to the yard run. The variety Cambridge Favourite, Elite strain is one that I recommend.

Vegetables Force rhubarb and seakale plants by covering the crowns with boxes or buckets and surrounding them with compost or straw manure. Gardeners in the north of England will probably sow broad beans this weekend, while those in the south will sow early peas, Brussels sprouts, spinach and summer cabbage. Kohlrabi is another more unusual vegetable which can be sown this weekend.

If you have finished picking Brussels sprouts, pull up the plants and smash the stems with the back of an axe before throwing them on the compost heap. In the south, in mild years, it is possible to sow onions and carrots now.

Greenhouse Sow the French bean Masterpiece in 15-cm (6-in) pots filled with compost; don't water until the plants are through. Plant cucumbers into their beds 90 cm (3 ft) apart. Prick out tomato seedlings into 7.5-cm (3-in) pots.

Sow lettuce seeds in boxes, and prick them out into boxes filled with compost. Treat seedlings of nemesias, lobelias, solanums, zinnias, salvias and browallias in the same way. Sow seeds of Russell lupins, delphiniums, tree lupins, China asters and scabious in boxes. Sow tomato seeds that are to be grown in a cold greenhouse or in the open. If chicory was not lifted earlier, it can now be forced under the staging of the greenhouse in heat and in the dark.

Pot on the large later-flowering chrysanthemums into 5-cm (6-in) pots. Rub out the weaker shoots of early vines, so as to leave only one good growth per spur. Titillate with a camelhair brush the early peach flowers, to distribute the pollen. Pot up the rooted cuttings of fuchsias into 7.5-cm (3-in) pots. Prune a greenhouse rose like Maréchal Niel quite severely.

March

In March, land must be cleared, and it may be necessary to lift crops like celery and leeks, and to heel the plants in closer together in an odd corner. Each week may bring greatly improved soil conditions, and keen amateur gardeners must seize opportunities as they occur. If March is really wet, then gardeners have to mark time.

Hardening off seedlings will be one important job. The plants will have been raised in boxes and pots, and they can now go into frames and under cloches.

First weekend
Flowers   It should be possible to replant and clean up an existing herbaceous border. Many perennials are better planted now than in the autumn. Delphiniums may need dividing; lift the plants carefully, cut them into three or four portions, and plant these pieces 90 cm (3 ft) apart. Sprinkle slug pellets over the soil among the plants to stop these pests from doing damage. Give the perennial scabious and gypsophila a dressing of lime – one handful per plant.

Fruit   If you want to graft apples and pears early in April, order grafting wax now. Order, too, the scions (one-year wood) from your nurseryman. It's a good thing to graft a pollinator on to a branch of a self-sterile tree. If blackcurrant bushes are showing swollen big buds, pick them off, drop them into a tin of paraffin and burn them. Dissolve 600 ml (1 pint) of lime-sulphur in 12 litres (19 pints) of water and spray the bushes with this solution when the majority of the leaves are the size of a 10p piece. You can spray any time between now and mid-April.

Colloidal sulphur may be used for preventing scab disease on apples and pears. Spray just before the blossoms open and immediately after the petals have fallen. Incidentally, this wash can also be used on rose bushes to prevent black spots.

Vegetables The mealy greenfly or aphis may do damage to cabbages and other brassicas; look under the leaves and, if you see pests, spray with liquid derris. Have a look at the earlier-sown row of parsnips, and if you can't see any seedlings, make a second sowing, choosing the variety The Student.

The leeks and onions sown in boxes in the greenhouse in January will need pricking out 2.5 cm (1 in) or more apart in new boxes. The earlier-sown tomatoes may need potting on from 7.5-cm (3-in) pots to 15-cm (6-in) ones.

Sow one of the salad onions like White Lisbon in shallow drills 30 cm (1 ft) apart. Don't thin the plants out – let them grow thickly and then pull them as you wish to use them.

Greenhouse Plan out the bedding scheme for your flower beds and then sow the seeds in No-Soil compost in boxes. Have plenty of holes in the bottoms of the boxes for drainage, and put some crocks over the holes before filling the boxes with compost.

Sow the seeds thinly on the firmed level compost, and sift a little more compost over the seeds to cover them. Press lightly with a wooden presser, water the seeds lightly and put the boxes on the staging of the greenhouse. Cover each box with a piece of glass and a sheet of newspaper, removing the glass each day to wipe it.

Second weekend

General Insect pests and diseases always seem to wake up at this time of the year, and the necessary precautions must be taken. If the weather is right, there will be a lot of seeds to be sown this week. If it's an early season, then there will be some pruning to do to climbers and hardy shrubs.

Flowers If you didn't plant your roses in the autumn, plant them now. Never plant deeply, but always plant firmly. If you mulch the ground with medium-grade sedge peat afterwards, the evaporation of moisture from the soil is prevented.

Feed the herbaceous border with fish manure at 50 g to the square metre (2 oz to the square yard). Add fine well-rotted compost to the border you are going to use for annuals. Rake it level afterwards and sow cornflowers, larkspur, clarkia, godetia, shirley poppies, mignonette and nasturtiums. Try out some of the more unusual annuals, too. If you sowed annuals in the autumn, now is the time to thin out the seedlings. Sow these annuals in unusually shaped drifts.

Shrubs and hedges   Plant flowering cherries, laburnums, pyrus and other flowering trees. Send an order to the nurseryman for evergreen shrubs to be planted in late April or early May. Give the shrub borders their dressing of sedge peat to the depth of 2.5 cm (1 in).

Fruit   Prune gooseberry bushes this weekend and spray them immediately afterwards to prevent the birds from pecking the buds. Mulch the newly planted fruit trees with compost or straw. Apply this for 90 cm (3 ft) around the trees. Keep the grease bands on apple and pear trees tacky by stirring the grease with a comb; this will catch the wingless females of the March moth. Birds may also be a nuisance on plums and pears, so spray the trees to make the buds unpleasant to the birds.

Vegetables   Though you can sow parsnips early, later sowings are less subject to canker. Sow a row now. Spinach can also be sown in a warm border outside, and leek seed can be sown in a seed bed to raise plants.

Radishes are a good salad crop; buy a packet of mixed varieties and you will have red, white, round roots, oval roots, long and short roots, and so on. Sow lettuce, early carrots and onions, putting three seeds in exactly where you want the plants to grow.

Sow broad beans (Longfellow variety) 7.5 cm (3 in) deep. Harden off the onion and leek plants that you raised in boxes in the greenhouse. If the weather wasn't right earlier, plant the very first early potatoes.

Greenhouse   If the autumn-sown cyclamen are growing well, pot them up into their 7.5-cm (3-in) plastic pots using No-Soil compost. Sit the corms firmly on the compost in the centre of each pot. Sow seeds of scented tobacco plants and French and African marigolds in boxes – also sow stocks, asters and petunias. No-Soil compost will prevent attack from the blackleg fungus.

Third weekend
General   If cleanliness is next to godliness, in the garden this refers

to tidiness, neatness and weedlessness. The efficient gardener gets his garden completely clean and tidy before the beginning of April. There are many seeds to be sown in the open, and unfortunately many pests and diseases to be kept at bay. Keep the garden medicine chest stocked.

Lawns   Continue to mow.

Flowers   Sow sweet peas, making certain to nick the seed cases of varieties whose skins are hard; try the plentiflora types which bear eight blooms on each stem. Lime the surface of the ground after sowing.

Sow seed of annuals like bells of Ireland, the spider flower, snow on the mountain, bartonia, and so on.

Fruit   Many varieties of apples, pears and plums are self-sterile – they need the pollen of another variety flowering at the same time to cause their blossoms to set. Family trees are ideal, for they provide their own pollinators.

The disease called scab can ruin the size and shape of apples and pears, so spray the trees with colloidal sulphur just before the blossoms open and after the blossoms have fallen. Buy colloidal sulphur now.

Vegetables   Plant out the cauliflowers you have been over-wintering in pots in a frame. Thin out the autumn-sown onions to about 15 cm (6 in) apart, transplanting some of them into new rows and using some now for salads. Sow Brussels sprouts, red cabbage, autumn cabbage and early savoys in a seed bed. If you live north of Manchester, sow sprouting broccoli as well. Sow leek seeds in a bed in the open, and sow a row of summer spinach.

Sow half a row of lettuces every weekend to get continuity – try Webbs Wonderful, Buttercrunch and Little Gem. (*plate 15*). Sow a row of an early variety of carrot and an early variety of turnip. Make the rows 30 cm (1 ft) apart. Do not thin out the carrots, but in a month's time thin out the turnips to 12 cm (5 in) apart.

Greenhouse   Sow seeds of large-flowered petunias in boxes – these are good for hanging baskets. Take stem cuttings of echeverias. Re-pot the calanthes. Take cuttings of fuchsias in No-Soil compost, and pot up the earlier-struck fuchsia cuttings into pots. Pot up the struck chrysanthemum cuttings into 15-cm (6-in) pots, while those that were potted up in February can be potted on into 15-cm (6-in) pots.

If you have been rooting begonia leaves, the little plants can now be potted up singly into 7.5-cm (3-in) pots, while the seedlings of verbenas, nemesias, petunias and begonias can be pricked out 2.5 cm (1 in) apart into boxes of compost.

Fourth weekend

General All rock garden lovers will be busy with their alpine plants. Dead leaves and other debris must be removed, many of the pockets will have to be dressed with fresh stone chippings, and labels will need renewing. Northerners will find that the lawns need mowing regularly from now on; people in the south of England will have been doing this for some time. Gardeners who have to cope with sticky soils in the north may still have to delay sowing, but all kinds of sowings may be made in light soils in the south.

Flowers Continue striking chrysanthemum cuttings and make all the dahlia cuttings that you can. Continue to sow annual flowers and mark out the drifts on raked, levelled land with a pointed stick. Where roses are not being grown on the sedge peat mulching principle, hoe the beds lightly and add fish manure at the same time, at 75 g to the square metre (3 oz to the square yard).

Plant lily bulbs and gladioli corms in groups of a dozen or so in a shrub or flower border. Sprinkle blue Draza pellets among delphiniums, lupins and pyrethrums to prevent attack by slugs. Give azaleas and rhododendrons a dressing of sedge peat all over the soil to a depth of 2.5 cm (1 in) if this has not been done already.

Fruit If you grow large dessert gooseberries, prune the leaders or one-year-old growths – cut them back by half and at the same time cut back the one-year-old side growths to within 7.5 cm (3 in) of their base. Spray afterwards to prevent attack from birds. Cut autumn-fruiting raspberries to within 15 cm (6 in) of the soil level.

Examine all staked fruit trees, and see that the plastic ties are secure but not too tight, and that the stakes are firm in the ground. Cut down below soil level any suckers coming up from the base of figs, peaches, nectarines and nuts. Watch out for American blight or woolly aphis on apple trees, and paint the affected parts with liquid derris.

Vegetables Hoe lightly through the rows of spring cabbages and lettuces. Plant lettuce seedlings on top of the celery trenches. Sow a row of early peas. Sow parsley as an edging to a bed. Sow seeds of sprouting broccoli, the various kales and the late savoys in a seed bed.

Order crowns of Regal pedigree asparagus for planting in April. One-year-old plants will do. Make up marrow beds or prepare places at the base of a fence where marrows and squashes can be planted to train upwards and take up little room. Sow a row of globe beetroot and another row of six-week turnips.

Always look out for club root disease, and prevent it by placing a piece of garlic in the hole at planting time.

Greenhouse Sow sweet corn seeds in boxes for planting out in May in the open. Sow balloon cos lettuce in boxes for planting out later. Sow Primula malacoides seed in compost so as to have plants in flower in November and December.

Divide the cannas to be used for bedding out. Take cuttings of plumbago capensis. Pot up rooted cuttings of alpine plants propagated in the autumn, and sow seed for other rock plants.

Apply a liquid manure to flowering deutzias, arums and pot roses. Bring the crinums into the greenhouse where they will get the maximum amount of light. Pot on thunias and take cuttings of sparmania and calanthe. Sow Gerbera jamesonii seed in boxes so as to have plants for putting out in the open in early summer.

Thin out the bunches of early grapes leaving only one bunch per lateral. Plant out some main-crop tomatoes in a border, or in pots to be grown on the ring culture system. The Eurocross variety is immune to mould disease. Seeds of this variety may be sown now for planting from the greenhouse in May.

April

April can be the busiest month of the year. There is a lot of seed sowing, and a fair amount of pruning to be done, and evergreens have to be planted. There are trees and climbers to move. It can, however, be a very showery month, as everyone knows, which may make it difficult for the gardener with limited time.

First weekend
General   Maybe you did prepare in March – and down came the rain or snow. So you may be behind – now is the time to catch up. Look back and see what you still have to do.

You will be hoeing constantly from now until the autumn – except on the beds where the sedge peat mulching has been done.

Lawns   Give the lawn a dressing of one of the hormone weedkillers. Make certain that this does not drift on to the flower border.

Flowers   Plant out early-flowering chrysanthemums and border carnations – though gardeners in the north may wait for a fortnight. If hardy annuals are growing well, thin them out and plant some of the thinnings into a reserve bed. Give the auriculas and polyanthus a feed of liquid manure – and repeat the dose next week. Hoe lightly around the plants.

Sow seed of the baby hardy annuals in little pockets in the rock garden. Plant out pentstemons and calceolarias where they are to flower. Plant out violas that have been wintering in the frames. Northerners may plant out sweet peas that were raised under glass.

Shrubs and hedges   Willows and dogwoods grown for coloured stems should be cut down to the ground. The tree of heaven (ailanthus glandulosus) grown as a bush can be treated in the same way, though the best effect is obtained from the large leaves and not from

31

GENERAL LAYERING

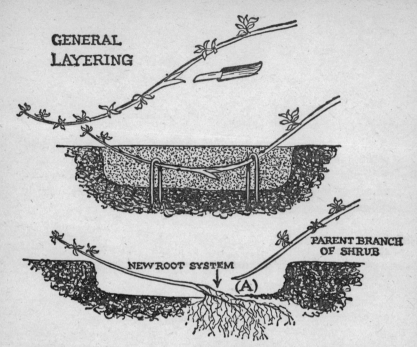

NEW ROOT SYSTEM

(A)

PARENT BRANCH OF SHRUB

Layering is best carried out in early spring or late summer, depending on the soil. Frequently shrubs such as rhododendrons, azaleas and magnolias will layer themselves. Where the new plant is severed from the parent plant is marked by 'A'

the stems. Late-flowering ceanothus, such as Gloire de Versailles, should be pruned now, all weak growths being cut out and last year's strong shoots reduced by half.

Fruit   This is the important month for spraying. Apples and pears must be sprayed, just before and after blossoming, with colloidal sulphur to prevent scab. If there are any signs of baby caterpillars or aphids, add liquid derris. It is usual to spray plums with liquid derris immediately after flowering to control red spider, and gooseberries should be sprayed with colloidal sulphur immediately after flowering to prevent American gooseberry mildew.

Vegetables   Plant the Regal one-year-old asparagus crowns in rows 90 cm (3 ft) apart, with the plants 75 cm (2 ft 6 in) apart in the rows.

In the south and south-west sow main crop carrots – variety James Scarlet Intermediate; sow this variety a week later in the Midlands, and a fortnight later in the north. Thin the onions to 15 cm (6 in) apart if you are growing a bulbing kind; if you are growing salad onions just start at the end of the row and pull what you need.

Sow more peas, spinach, turnips and carrots if desired. Sow kohl-rabi, and eat the roots when they are the size of tennis balls. Northern gardeners should sow broad beans and lettuce.

Greenhouse Pinch back the ends of melon shoots at one leaf beyond each fruit. Pollinate the female blooms with a camel-hair brush full of male pollen.

Sow seeds of the runner bean Scarlet Emperor in compost in boxes, to have plants to put out in mid-May. Sow seeds of the Conqueror cucumber to raise plants for putting out in frames next month. Sow seeds of the various squashes in 7.5-cm (3-in) pots. Make up hot beds for melons and cucumbers in unheated frames.

Second weekend

General Gardeners with light soils will appreciate April rain because they can soon get to work on sandy land after a shower. When plants are grown on the mulching principle, i.e. if straw is 30 cm (1 ft) deep all over the ground where the soft fruits are growing, it is possible to spray or prune even after heavy rain. If rosebeds are covered with sedge peat 2.5 cm (1 in) deep, a gardener can get on them without ruining the soil half an hour after the rain has stopped.

Flowers Many perennials can be propagated this weekend by cutting off basal growths that are now being produced around the clumps. These can be dibbled into sandy soil in a shady spot. If you then cover them with cloches or Access frames, they will soon start to grow and make good plants.

Get over the rust problem in hollyhocks by planting out one-year-old seedlings each season. Put the plants in firmly at the back of the border. Go over flower borders to see whether there are any gaps caused by the late frost, and if so fill them up.

Prune the roses this weekend, or at any rate make a start, so that by the end of the month all the rose pruning will have been carried out. Plant out aquilegias, thalictrums and most of the hardy primulas.

Shrubs and hedges Dwarf conifers are attractive, and their pinnacle shapes make them a useful foil to trailing plants. Plant them now.

Fruit Train nectarberries, blackberries and boysenberries against walls, fences, or the special wires that you have provided for them. The old wood must be cut away altogether, and the young wood trained in a fan-like shape. Go down the rows of raspberries and, if there are more than five or six good strong canes per clump, thin them out.

This is a good week-end for grafting. Many gardeners will take the opportunity of top-grafting any self-sterile varieties in the garden with a suitable pollinator. Graft one of the branches in this way to provide all the male pollen needed.

Freshen the sticky compound on the tree bands this weekend, either by adding a little more of the tacky material or by scraping the band once again with an old comb. Keeping looking out for the white woolly colonies of American blight or woolly aphis, and paint these immediately with neat liquid derris.

Vegetables Sow seeds of savoys, sprouting broccoli and the various kales in a specially prepared seedbed (*plate 6*). Also put in the seed of the later summer cabbage varieties such as Greyhound. Salsify is an unusual and delicious root vegetable that ought to be grown more. Put in a row this weekend to try it. Thin the seedlings out to 15 cm (6 in) apart.

Plant the early varieties of potatoes, especially those that have been well sprouted. If any tubers are too big, cut them in two. In some of the milder areas you may have been able to plant them a fortnight ago. If you have had scab on the tubers in the past, put some fresh grass mowings in the drills and there will be no more trouble. Some people will want to plant later varieties also, because they need a long season of growth.

Greenhouse Propagate the large-flowered mimulus by cuttings, which root quickly. Also take cuttings of the plumbago, deutzia, ceratostigma, abutilon, epacris and cytisus. Look at the clivias and re-pot those that need it. Pot up the tuberous-rooted begonias into the pots in which they are to flower. Also pot on ivy-leaved geraniums.

Start the dahlias off if the aim is to plant stools and not to take cuttings. Put the stools into a box of dampish sedge peat and stand the box on the staging of the greenhouse. Divide and pot up lobelia fulgens and you will have good plants for putting out in late May.

When the days are really sunny you can take the frame lights off the frames where carrots, turnips, lettuces and early potatoes are growing. This will give them a really good airing. Be sure to put the lights back when the sun goes down, so that the plants have the right protection at night.

Sow some more early dwarf beans in a 15-cm (6-in) pot filled with compost. Space six seeds evenly around the edge of the pot, 2.5 cm (1 in) deep. Thin down to four plants later. Plant out marrows into frames over a mild hot bed. Set out one plant in the centre of a 2-metre by 1.25-metre (6-ft by 4-ft) frame. The plan is to train the laterals out to the four corners.

Third weekend
General This is a great weekend for the firm planting of evergreen flowering shrubs. It is also a good weekend for rose pruning. The newcomer may be muddled by two schools of thought – the hard pruners and those that merely tip. Pruning invariably has to be learned the hard way; a good general rule covering both fruit trees and roses is to be careful and very moderate. If you don't prune at all you will get some results, but if you seriously overprune there may be disaster.

Flowers Plant out the perennials and biennials that you have raised in the greenhouse and hardened off in the frames where they are to grow. Give them plenty of room, and if the weather is dry give them a good watering.

Cut back the dead flowers on the rock garden plants the moment they cease to be at their best. This stops them going to seed and saves unnecessary exhaustion. Rampant varieties – e.g. aubrietias and arabis – may also be cut back hard now.

Some people never bother to start dahlia tubers off under glass. They store carefully in the winter, split them up at this time of the year and plant them out now. Give the tubers plenty of room – if a variety is known to grow 120 cm (4 ft) high, give it 60 cm (2 ft) of room on either side, and if it grows to 90 cm (3 ft) high, leave only 45 cm (18 in) on either side.

Shrubs and hedges   There may be some shrubs to prune this weekend. The general rule is to cut back specimens the moment blossoming is over, and this particularly applies to forsythia.

Fruit   Continue spraying apples and pears as necessary, using colloidal sulphur. The main spraying is done at the pink blossom stage, i.e. just before the flowers open, in the case of apples (*plate 1*), and at the white blossom stage in the case of pears. The next major spraying period is at the moment the blossoms have fallen. It is a good idea to spray when 80 per cent of the blossoms have fallen, and then you can add to the wash a little liquid pyrethrum-derris, at the rate of say 25 g to 45 litres (1 oz to 10 gal). The aim is to kill apple sawflies, which may cause maggots in the apples. Give the trees a thorough soaking from top to toe on a nice, dry day.

Vegetables   Sow one or two rows of long beet, choosing the varieties Long Blood Red or Covent Garden. You can also put in one or two rows of the quick-growing round beet, like Boltardy. Give the peas their sticks this weekend, or provide the rows with wire netting up which the plants can climb. If you want very large onions for show, plant out the seedlings in rows 30 cm (1 ft) apart, with 20 cm (8 in) between the plants. The variety Ailsa Craig is good for this purpose. Plant firmly but shallowly – the roots must be in the ground, but the white part of the plant must just sit on the soil level.

Prepare your celery trench, if you have not done so already. When the ridges are properly made, plant out lettuce seedlings on top or, if you prefer, sow a row of French beans here instead. If you want to raise globe artichokes sow the seed now, under frames or continuous cloches, very shallowly, or in compost in a frame.

This is a good weekend to sow French beans, except perhaps in the most exposed positions in the north. Draw out the drills 5 cm (2 in) deep and 45 cm (18 in) apart, and space the seeds out 12 cm (5 in) apart in the rows. Choose a variety like Processor.

Greenhouse   Plant a young vine this weekend in the greenhouse.

This will come container-grown from the nurseryman, so there will be the minimum of root disturbance. Plant firmly, spreading the roots out evenly, and then cut the rod down to within 45 cm (18 in) of soil level, just above a bud, after planting. If you have vines growing in a border apply fish manure with a 10 per cent potash content, at 100 g to the square metre (4 oz to the square yard), and hoe it lightly in.

Fourth weekend

General   There is a tendency at the end of April to feel that every-thing is safe. It may be so mild that you cannot imagine there could possibly be a frost. Do not be tempted to plant out the tender speci-mens, either flowers or fruit, until the middle of May. I have known trouble later than this. If potato shoots are coming through the soil it is a good idea to earth them up to keep them covered; later, when it is safe, you can hoe down the deep sides of the drills again.

Flowers   Finish pruning the roses, rake up the prunings, put them on the compost heap and sprinkle them with a fish fertilizer. There should be some grass mowings at this time of the year which should go in with the prunings to help rot them down. Mark for propagation the best coloured polyanthuses, primroses, and coloured cowslips; just put a little label by the plants that you think are worth keeping and splitting up.

Plant out antirrhinums where you want them to grow. If you have had trouble with rust in the past, choose one of the resistant varieties.

The bulbous flowers should now be showing themselves. Cut any of the blooms that you need in the house, and watch those that you leave, so that you can cut off their heads before they go to seed. Treat pansies and violas in the same manner. You will find that if you keep on cutting off the faded flowers week after week the plants will go on blooming much longer. Sow annuals either in serried lines for cutting, or in drifts in a flower border. Get hold of a good catalogue, and try some of the more unusual kinds.

Shrubs and hedges   If you have a shrub euonymus europaeus, spray it with liquid derris this weekend, because it is on this shrub that the black fly breeds before it goes on to the broad beans.

Fruit   If you forgot to spray peaches and nectarines with colloidal sulphur in February, pick off all the leaves showing leaf curl damage and burn them. Early fruit trees growing against walls often suffer from dryness at the roots at this time of the year. So flood the borders in order to prevent any trouble during blossoming. Many flowers fail to set properly because of dryness at the roots.

If you have had trouble with big bud on your blackcurrants spráy the bushes with lime-sulphur, at the rate of 600 ml to 11 litres (1 pint to 19 pints) of water, as already mentioned. Spray just before the blossoms open, and give the bushes a thorough soaking.

Vegetables Make a big sowing of onions on well-manured and really firm land. Choose a variety like Dura. The tomato seedlings should now be ready to be potted up into their 7.5-cm (3-in) plastic pots. These produce good specimens for planting out in the open about the middle of May. Sow a row or two of a quick-hearting cabbage like Greyhound or Vienna Baby Head to ensure succession. Pinch out the growing points of the first-sown row of broad beans, to discourage the ravages of the black fly. Don't forget what has already been said about earthing up potatoes to protect the young new shoots.

Greenhouse If you have peaches under glass give them plenty of ventilation during the next week or two, while the fruits are swelling. Keep a sharp lookout for red spider – keep this down by regularly spraying the under-surface of the leaves with liquid derris. Take cuttings of salvias, jacobinias, eupatoriums and lasiandras or tibouchinas.

Clarkias and schizanthus should now be growing well and will need staking and tying. The cannas will want potting on into their 12-cm (5-in) pots and the chrysanthemums into 15-cm (6-in) pots. Save fire heat and so reduce the greenhouse temperatures wherever possible. Ventilation may be increased from now on. In the south and south-west it is often necessary to use shading on the glass from the end of April onwards.

May

May is a dangerous month. It is often sunny and dry, and gardeners are tempted to put out plants which are not quite hardy. In the south I have known serious frosts about the middle of the month, and in the north as late as June.

First weekend
General It is never safe to put out tomatoes until the end of the second week, although quite a number of gardeners do so and get away with it. April showers may have brought on the potatoes, but play safe and protect the tops in spite of the warmer weather.

Lawns Trim the verges regularly, and keep the lawns well mowed. A motor mower saves a lot of back-breaking work.

Flowers Sow wallflower seeds, as well as the seeds of canterbury bells, hollyhocks, forget-me-nots, honesty, sweet william, evening primroses and scabious. It is possible to propagate wallflowers from cuttings, but it is only really necessary in the case of double varieties.

The April-sown annuals need thinning out now. Sow the seeds of half-hardy annuals such as browallia, celosia, portulaca, rhodanthe out of doors. Peg down ivy-leaved geraniums, make them trail over the ground properly and re-root them at the pegged points.

As greenhouse bulbs finish flowering, plant them out in the orchard around the fruit trees. Make them look as natural as possible. A good way of doing this is to toss a handful on the ground and plant the bulbs where they fall.

Fruit Carry out normal pruning, i.e. cut back the laterals by about half. Bark ringing can be carried out if your trees are making too much wood instead of fruiting.

Some of the spraying work that should normally have been done last month may have to be done now. The main apple blossoming period usually takes place in the first half of this month and, as a result, post-blossom spraying for scab, red spider and sawfly has to be carried out. Use colloidal sulphur, liquid derris and pyrethrum. For sawfly on plums, give a really thorough soaking with liquid derris this weekend. Wall trees and particularly cherries and redcurrants are prone to black aphids at this time of the year, and they too can be sprayed with a strong liquid derris.

Vegetables The seeds of vegetable marrows, squashes, pumpkins and gourds can be sown in the open provided the spot where they are sown is covered with an upturned jamjar. Prepare the spot where the seeds are going to be sown by digging a hole at least a spade's depth and a spade's width, and burying in the bottom some well-rotted compost. Then put the earth back, and sow three seeds on the top of the mound you have formed. The compost creates heat which will help the young seedlings and provide some food for the growing plant later. If all the seeds germinate, thin out to one in each position. Each planting should be at least 90 cm (3 ft) from the next.

Make a sowing of maincrop peas this weekend. Make the rows 90 cm (3 ft) apart as a general rule, though the taller kinds may need 1.2 metres (4 ft) between the rows. In heavy soils the drills should be 5 cm (2 in) deep and in lighter sandy soils 7.5 cm (3 in). Space the seeds out 7.5 cm (3 in) apart in a zigzag fashion, and when they come through protect them from the birds with black cotton strung from one end of the row to the other. If you have trouble with mice, use the kind of traps that break their backs, and bait them with marrow seeds. It is best to use sticks for the peas to climb up but fish netting or wire netting can be used as an alternative.

Greenhouse Propagate heaths from cuttings now. They strike well in almost pure sandy soil, particularly if you give them a little heat. Put rooted perpetual-flowering carnations into the cold frame. Stake, feed and syringe those that are to grow under glass the whole of the spring and summer.

Pot on zonal pelargoniums into the 15-cm (6-in) pots in which they will flower during the winter. After 10 days you can put them outside on cinders until the autumn, when they will have to be brought in again. During the summer pinch out the flower trusses as they form.

Chrysanthemums in pots can also be put out of doors now, but make sure they are in a sheltered position, and watch out for frosts. If you stretch a wire between two posts, and tie canes to the wire, the plants, attached to the stakes, will not blow over in the wind when they are growing well.

Second weekend
General   Cloches and Access frames are useful this month – use them over dahlias, begonias and chrysanthemums which you have put outside. Glass coverage makes all the difference if there is a frost, as plants will not be damaged. Keep weeds down this month by hoeing, and continue regular hoeing until early June so as to avoid trouble for the rest of the season. Just hoe through the top 1 cm ($\frac{1}{2}$ in) – there is no need to go deeper – to produce what is called a dust mulch.

Any kind of mulch helps to retain moisture in the ground. Use sedge peat this month as a top dressing 2.5 cm (1 in) deep for shrubs, soft fruits, herbaceous plants and so on. These mulchings help to smother weeds.

Flowers   If you live in the Midlands or north, this is likely to be a good weekend for planting out the early-flowering chrysanthemums. Those who want more violets should propagate them by cuttings this weekend. Winter bedding plants will need to come out now to make room for the summer bedding. Rake in a fish manure at the rate of 7.5 cm (3 oz) to the square yard when preparing the soil.

If you have a shady border, plant divided cowslips, primroses and polyanthuses, provided, of course, they have finished flowering. You will then have some more nice plants to put out in the autumn.

You should be able now to plant out your half-hardy annuals, such as nemesias, asters and stocks. You can plant out more gladioli corms for succession, and put out some of the more tender bedding plants in the frames for hardening off, ready to be planted out next weekend.

Fruit   About the twelfth of this month spray loganberries with colloidal sulphur to prevent cane spot. Treat the raspberries in the same way. This spraying should be done just before they bloom, which is usually about the third week in May.

Did you do any grafting in April? If so, examine them carefully, and if the cambium layers have knitted together successfully, remove the raffia. At the same time rub off any shoots growing below the graft.

Vegetables If the potatoes are through, give them another slight earthing up to protect them from frost. Hoe some of the soil down once all risk of frost is past. Sow another row of lettuce for succession. Make a sowing of French beans if the soil is warm enough. Masterpiece is a good variety. Northerners can sow one or two rows of swedes, 45 cm (18 in) apart.

A small border for growing herbs is very useful. Plant it, for convenience, near the kitchen door. Parsley is easily grown from seed. Plant rows of mint 22.5 cm (9 in) apart. There are various kinds – lemon mint, apple mint, spearmint, etc. – each with its own particular flavour. Sage will root without any difficulty, but make sure that your cutting has a heel to it. Thyme can be grown from seed or from cuttings. The plants should eventually be 15 cm (6 in) apart in the row, with the rows 30 cm (1 ft) apart. Other herbs which may be added include tarragon, rue and sorrel.

Sow the seed of the tiny cabbage known as Golden Acre Primo where you want the plants to grow, and thin out later to 20 or 22 cm (8 or 9 in) apart. Summer cabbages can be planted out where they are to crop. Put them out 60 cm (2 ft) square, on well-manured land. Feed the onions, if they are growing well, by applying fish manure at 25 g to the metre (1 oz to the yard) run. Follow this by a light hoeing.

Greenhouse Syringe over cyclamens at least once a day. They do not like bright sunlight, so see that they are shaded from it. The primulas which you are keeping as pot plants can be put into the cold frames now; those you do not want to keep can be put on the compost heap, and the pots washed and put away. Sow cineraria seed in boxes filled with compost. Cinerarias should be grown on slowly.

Stake your herbaceous calceolarias, for they should now be growing quite well. You may also need to tie up some plants with raffia. If you want to make a hanging basket, obtain a suitable wire basket and line it well with moss. You can then plant it with trailing lobelias and ivy-leaved geraniums, or with asparagus ferns and salvias. Other plants will, of course, suggest themselves to you, and with a little thought these baskets can be made most attractive.

Third weekend

General Regular hoeing should start to keep down weeds and provide a dust mulch. A dutch hoe is the gardener's best friend after sedge peat mulch. Weeds can be controlled more easily while they are still small seedlings, so attack them thoroughly this weekend.

Though it is true to say that all evergreens, including conifers, may be moved during the weekend, follow the planting by careful syringing from time to time if a dry spell follows. Water them plentifully.

Lawns Give the lawn some attention now, if it has not previously been fed. Some people use lawn sand at 75-100 g to the square metre (3-4 oz to the square yard), applying it dry so that it burns up the broader leaves of the weeds but feeds the grasses (*plate 11*). It is, however, dangerous to apply this too heavily, except perhaps where there are large patches of weeds. As an alternative, use a liquid hormone weedkiller like Verdone. Again, be careful in applying it. Keep the rose of your watering-can near the ground so that the spray does not drift on to the flower borders. You can then feed the grass with fish manure at 50-75 g to the square metre (2-3 oz to the square yard).

Flowers Make sure all border plants are sufficiently staked. Use twiggy sticks in between the annuals and most of the perennials, pushing them in close to the plants which will then grow up and hide them. While you are doing this, look out for off-shoots from the perennials. These, when severed with a sharp knife, can conveniently be struck in sandy soil in a shady spot.

Fruit Disbud peaches and nectarines if they are making plenty of shoots. The fruits on the apricots should be thinned to only one fruit every 7.5 cm (3 in). Any other thinning can be carried out later, after the stones have formed. Wall trees can get very dry towards the end of May, so water them well if necessary. If your trees are troubled with red spider, syringe the leaves on their under-sides with liquid derris.

Shoots will be starting to come up in the raspberry rows. Start to thin these out now, especially if you have the strong-growing Malling Promise, Malling Jewel or other similar variety. Plum trees, nut trees and others may also have suckers coming up which you should grub up. If you have put any hessian-like material in front of your wall trees to protect them, remove this now and dry it. You can then put it away to be used again next year.

Vegetables   Late savoys are useful, particularly Ormskirk Late. Prepare a seed bed by raking into the soil damped sedge peat, together with fish manure at the rate of 50 g to the square metre (2 oz to the square yard). At the same time hydrated lime can be applied to the surface in the same proportions. Make out drills 1 cm ($\frac{1}{2}$ in) deep, and 15 cm (6 in) apart, for your seed sowing. An unusual vegetable known as couve tronchuda can be planted out now in rows 60 cm (2 ft) apart. Use the thick, white stems as seakale and the dark green leaves as cabbage.

Runner beans are a great standby and most people like to have more than one row. Remember, however, that you can have them growing up poles in circles, or you can train them up wire netting or string. The rows should be 1.75 metres (6 ft) apart, but if the plants are cut back now and again with a pair of shears they need only be 90 cm (3 ft) apart. Sow the beans about 5 cm (2 in) deep and 15 cm (6 in) apart in the rows.

Cucumber plants grow well now if they are put in a garden frame. Melons – variety Dutch Net (*plate* 8) – can also go out. If ridge cucumbers are preferred, sow the seed of Burpee Hybrid where it is to grow. This variety is long, dark green and smooth skinned. You can also sow the seeds of bush marrows and squashes where you want them to mature, without having to cover them in glass.

If you want to force some seakale in heat in the winter, then disbud it now so that there is only one good growth left per crown. If you like chicory and cultivated dandelions in your salad bowl, sow these seeds now in rows 45 cm (15 in) apart for forcing in the winter. Later on the plants should be thinned out to one every foot or so in the row.

Greenhouse   Towards the end of the month we often have more sunshine, and if this is the case more ventilation can be given. Unfortunately, this often increases pest trouble, especially from aphids and thrips. It may be necessary to use a smoke to penetrate the hidden cracks and crevices of the greenhouse where pests may be lurking.

The older cyclamen plants that have finished flowering can now be dried off gradually, although some people plant them out in a frame.

Chrysanthemums will need to be repotted for the last time. See to the exhibition varieties first if you intend to put them in for a show.

Fourth weekend

Flowers Remove the dead heads of flowers to prevent them from going to seed. To prolong the flowering period, keep cutting them for the house. Cut down the earlier-flowering herbaceous plants, as they finish blooming, to within 15 cm (6 in) of ground level. Remove the seed heads from rhododendrons and azaleas, which will make them bloom much better the following season.

Put out now where they are to flower the more tender bedding plants, i.e. marguerites and calceolarias, zonal pelargoniums, cannas and the glorious blue salvia patens. Try to complete the bedding by the end of this month, but leave 'cherry pie' and dahlias until the end, just in case there should be any frost.

Fruit The rows of strawberries should be hoed lightly to keep down the weeds, and sedge peat should be put down as a mulch. This is excellent for keeping the berries clean. Some people use straw instead, but sedge peat is better because it contains no weed seeds and discourages slugs. The plants appreciate the organic matter when it is left in position.

After peating, cover the strawberry plants with nylon netting as a protection from birds. If the weather is very dry, flood the ground before applying peat.

Vegetables Sow more lettuce to continue the supply. It pays to put them in at intervals of about 10 days.

Sow another variety of maincrop peas, choosing a variety like Meteor or the dwarf Onward. Once a week sow a few radishes, using a packet of mixed seed in preference to one variety.

The main batch of celery needs to be planted out now, 30 cm (1 ft) apart in the rows, and rows 90 cm (3 ft) apart. The end of May may be a dry period, and if so vegetables will need watering. Some crops, such as peas, benefit greatly from this.

Do not leave your old cabbage stumps in the ground, for they rob it of food and form a breeding ground for pests. Grub them up immediately, and crush the hard stems with the back of an axe. They will then rot down easily on the compost heap and make excellent manure.

This is a wonderful time for all the pests that attack your garden produce, so keep a sharp lookout for them, and spray with the right insecticide at the right time. Black fly may attack broad beans any time now, so spray the plants with liquid derris or pyrethrum when these pests are first seen.

Greenhouse If you want to propagate some hydrangea hortensis, then make cuttings now. The small-leaved rhododendrons can also be increased by cuttings this weekend. Make a horizontal cut just below a node, trim off the lower leaves, and push the cutting into sandy soil. It is usual at this time to bring the amaryllis into warmth to make it start growing.

June

In June many of the winter occupants of the greenhouse can be brought out. All fear of frost is past, and so out come potted shrubs such as azaleas, camellias, genistas, acacias, and the winter cherries. Pots may be plunged up to their rims in a sheltered position out of doors. There they can be kept well watered and syringed – syringing will keep down red spider.

First weekend

Flowers   If it is hot this weekend, water annuals thoroughly. Sprinklers do this better than a watering can. To be effective, a rain sprinkler must be left in one position for at least half an hour. It is all right to water in the sun, provided the water is thrown well up into the air.

Gladioli are very beautiful, especially the butterfly types. Plant corms straight away. They will follow those that were planted earlier in May, and you will have continuous flowers for cutting for the house. If you haven't yet sown wallflowers, forget-me-nots or alyssum you can sow the seeds now. For a show of Brompton stocks in March, sow the seeds now in a well-prepared seed bed. Raise new hollyhock plants every year, because the old ones suffer badly from rust – sow seeds at this time of year.

Fruit   If apples and pears are to be pruned on the Lorette pruning method, start this month. The laterals are cut to within 3 mm ($\frac{1}{8}$ in) of their base when they have reached the half-ripened stage, and are about 20 or 22 cm (8 or 9 in) long. Apples and pears treated this way respond splendidly. Thin the apples at the same time. Cut them off with scissors, so that the remaining fruits are at an average distance apart of 10 cm (4 in). With cooking varieties, which grow longer, they need to be at least 15 cm (6 in) apart.

Look at your plum trees, and see if you need to thin the fruit. If you leave on all the plums there may be a breakdown crop, and the branches will be broken. This often allows silver leaf disease to enter.

The fruitlets should be thinned out to 2.5 cm (1 in) apart. In the case of the heavier-cropping kinds like the Victoria, thin to 5 or even 7.5 cm (2 or even 3 in) apart. Gooseberries are thinned as they are picked. Look at your outdoor grapevine, and thin the fruits. Remove as many as 50 per cent of the berries.

Vegetables Sow summer spinach in rows 30 cm (1 ft) apart. Thin the plants out later on to 15 cm (6 in) apart in the rows. Spinach has a habit of going to seed but, if you fork plenty of dampened sedge peat into the ground first at a bucketful to the metre (yard) run, the peat holds the moisture until the roots of the plants need it, and as a result seeding does not take place so quickly. As it is important to ensure quick germination, soak the spinach seed in water before sowing.

If you find spinach indigestible try eating perpetual spinach or seakale spinach, or even a plant known as New Zealand spinach, which was discovered by Captain Cook. This needs 90 cm (3 ft) in which to grow, as it spreads over the ground. The first two can be sown 45 cm (18 in) apart, with 45 cm (18 in) also between the rows.

Cautious gardeners who have not yet put out their tomato and cucumber plants may safely do so now. If you prefer to buy in plants, make certain to get sturdy short-jointed dark green specimens, rather than the long lanky plants which never give good results.

Greenhouse Continue to pot on chrysanthemums into their final pots. The echeverias, solanums and crotons are probably large enough to be potted up into their 15-cm (6-in) pots. If winter-flowering wallflowers are required for greenhouse decoration, sow the seed now in compost.

Seedling cyclamens may now be ready to be potted up into 7.5-cm (3-in) pots, and primula seedlings can be treated in the same manner. Zonal pelargoniums can go into their flowering pots at the same time. Protect hippeastrums from thrips by giving them a dusting of derris – they often suffer from this pest at this time of the year.

Second weekend
Flowers Take cuttings of arabis, aubrietia and alyssum. They only need to be about 2.5 cm (1 in) long – dibble them into sandy soil in a fairly shady spot. Some perennials do well when raised from seed and these can be sown now. Go to a seedsman who specializes in this kind

of seed. If you have already sown perennials, the seedlings may need to be planted out into reserve beds, 10 cm (4 in) apart. Keep watering the annuals if the weather is warm.

Fruit   Flood rows of raspberries well. Give them a good mulching with straw, well-rotted compost or sedge peat afterwards. Lawn mowings are a useful substitute. Treated in this way, the raspberries will swell properly. The growths on nectarines and peaches should be regularly trained from now on. Remove those that are not required either for manufacturing sap to plump up the fruits or as replacements in the winter.

If you put bands of corrugated cardboard (corrugations on the inside) or sacking around the trunks of the fruit trees, the larvae of the codling moth will be caught as they go down to pupate. Codling moth maggots attack apples at this time of the year.

Very often strawberries are attacked by mildew in dry weather. The answer is to water them well, so that they will be in a strong condition to resist these attacks. Trees growing against walls may suffer from lack of moisture at this time of year, and it is often necessary to give them a good flooding.

Vegetables   If you like French beans, make a second sowing of them now. Choose stringless types, which are quicker to prepare. Processor is a good stringless variety.

In a shady spot sow a quick-maturing type of turnip. First of all work into the ground plenty of well-damped sedge peat to hold the moisture in the ground. Make the rows 45 cm (18 in) apart. Later on, thin out the plants to 12 cm (5 in) apart.

Sow cucumbers out of doors this weekend. The seeds should be planted 90 cm (3 ft) apart, and 2.5 cm (1 in) deep. Put in two or three seeds in each position. Thin them out to one per position later on, provided they all germinate. A jamjar over the seeds helps them to germinate quicker, and can be removed later on. A flower pot may be used instead, provided it is not left on too long.

Stop cutting asparagus about now, and give the rows a dressing of well-rotted compost at two bucketsful to the metre (yard) run.

Greenhouse   Complete the final potting up of your chrysanthemums. No-Soil compost may be put round the earlier-sown cucumbers as a top-dressing. Pot up and stake fuchsias. Stake thunias and plant gloxinia seedlings, which should be about 2.5 cm (1 in) high, into 7.5-cm (3-in) pots. Seedlings of tuberous begonias should be potted up into No-Soil compost at the same time.

There is a winter-flowering type of forget-me-not which can be grown under glass. Sow the seed out of doors in a semi-shady place this week. A batch of cucumber seed can also be sown in compost. The earlier cucumbers should need training and tying in, while the earlier tomatoes need to be dis-shooted and either tied to bamboos or twisted round the strings you have provided. Plant tomatoes under glass if you want a late crop.

Third weekend

General If you have not yet made up your mind to adopt the mulching system, June is a very good month to do so and start. Light hoeing is still important – if you keep the garden free from weeds right the way through to the end of this month, you will hardly have any weeds for the rest of the year. It ought to be possible to plant out tender subjects during June, for frost is very rare now.

Lawns Keep mowing your lawns regularly. Water them now with a selective weedkiller.

Flowers June is the month for cut roses and sweet peas, and the more you cut them, the better they crop. If the anchusas, delphiniums and lupins have finished flowering, cut them down almost to ground level. Give them plenty of water, and a good mulching of sedge peat or compost, and you should get a second show of blooms in September.

If annuals like clarkia and godetia are to branch out properly, instead of having one long straggly stem, you must now pinch out the tops. Sweet williams can be propagated by cuttings, as well as the best of the pansies and sweet rockets. Propagate pinks by pipings. Insert them in sandy soil, and they should root easily.

Shrubs and hedges Azaleas, rhododendrons and other shrubs that have finished flowering should have their seeding heads removed.

Fruit Give strawberries another watering if the soil is dry. They should be ready for picking now – gather them as soon as they are ripe, or the slugs and the birds will get them. To keep the berries clean, use sedge peat as a mulch. There should be gooseberries to pick, and redcurrants too. If your pears have got scab, spray the trees with colloidal sulphur.

Use a derris-pyrethrum wash for morello cherries growing on a north wall or fence. This is the best way to control the black fly or aphis which attacks at this time of year. See if caterpillars are attacking your gooseberries, and if so spray the bushes with a solution of liquid derris. Spray the raspberries with a similar wash, in order to prevent maggoty fruit. Little beetles may be about at this time, laying their eggs in the flowers, and it is these eggs which hatch out into maggots.

Vegetables Many gardeners will be harvesting early potatoes now. Another crop which should be ready is the early cauliflower, together with Primata cabbages and well-hearted lettuce.

The carrots sown last month will need thinning now. Progressive thinning is good because you can eat nice young carrots now and leave others to grow larger. The fern tops of the asparagus should now be left to grow naturally.

Cardoons should be planted in the open – they like to grow in trenches like celery. Celeriac can also be planted. Early savoys, late savoys, kale and broccoli should be planted out if this has not already been done. If you have had trouble with cabbage root maggot in the past, put into the holes a piece of garlic the size of a French bean when planting.

Greenhouse If you want to grow strawberries under glass for the new year fill 7.5-cm (3-in) pots with No-Soil potting compost. Sink these in the ground in the open, next to healthy one-year-old Cambridge Favourite (Elite strain) plants. Strike the runners directly into the pots. If the first batch of tomatoes is finished, remake the bed and replant as soon as possible. The other tomatoes, and the cucumbers, can be trained up stakes or strings as they continue to grow.

There is a lot of potting on to do. The saintpaulia should go into 15-cm (6-in) pots, and so should the buddleia asiatica and the begonia semperflorens. 7.5-cm (3-in) pots should be used for potting on coleus. The chrysanthemums may be attacked by aphids so watch out. Spray with liquid derris immediately you see them – you can use the same wash as for the morello cherries.

Fourth weekend

General Keep a wary eye open for caterpillars, aphids and other pests. If they get established and multiply unchecked, they can create havoc. Modern sprays dissolve quickly in water and can be used with great success. Always read the instructions on the container before applying. Attend to the general staking and tying also, so that plants don't flop on the ground. Use a liquid manure for feeding the various flowering plants which are in bud and in bloom.

Flowers Have a look at the rock garden and made sure that the more rampant growers are not restricting the growth of the more choice specimens. Some of the plants can be propagated by seed sowing. The seeds normally germinate best when they are sown almost immediately.

Border carnations, and any perpetual-flowering kinds that you are growing in the open should be disbudded from time to time. Look for suckers on roses and cut them out.

Put in an order now for the bulbs you will soon want to plant – colchicums, autumn crocuses, sternbergias, erythroniums and hardy cyclamens. Don't forget the lovely madonna and nankeen lilies which should be ordered at the same time.

Shrubs and hedges Cutting off suckers is an important job. Lilacs and rhododendrons are especially prone to this.

Fruit Give the apple trees another spraying with a solution of pyrethrum against codling moth maggots. Dwarf walnut trees should be summer pruned, both now and again in July. Pinch out about 1 cm ($\frac{1}{2}$ in) of the tips of the young growing shoots when not more than six leaves have been formed. This makes the buds below the stopped tip plump up and become female flower buds. Do not touch the thin weak shoots, as these bear the male pollen catkins.

Examine blackcurrant bushes for reversion. If any bushes have been attacked by this virus disease, mark them with a cane and make sure they are grubbed up and burned immediately when the fruit has all been picked.

Redcurrants should be brutted this weekend. This means that half of each lateral is broken off with the back of a pocket-knife. By breaking them in this way you let light and air into the bushes to help ripen the fruit, and the fruit buds for next year's cropping. Further secondary growth, as it is called, is prevented.

Vegetables Mulch runner beans and peas with sedge peat or lawn mowings to conserve the moisture. Take care not to heap lawn mowings on too deeply, or they will heat up and damage the stems. The early peas should be pulled up as soon as they have finished cropping, so that you can use the land for another crop. Make sure that the later peas are sticked in time. If you neglect to do this in the early stages, they may topple over and you will probably get a poorer crop.

Give the bulbing onions a dressing of fish manure, with a 10 per cent potash content, at 50 g to the metre (2 oz to the yard) run. Dust the young turnips, as they come through, with derris-pyrethrum to prevent attacks of flea beetle. Transplant some of the beetroot seedlings to fill up the gaps; water well afterwards. The marrow supply can be kept going by cutting the fruits when they are half size.

Greenhouse Sow seeds of the miniature white nicotiana, for these make charming winter-flowering plants. Cineraria seed can be sown for spring flowering, and the Indian azaleas which should have finished flowering can be put out on to the standing ground to rest.

Large late chrysanthemums should now be standing out on ashes, somewhere near the greenhouse. The plants should be tied to their canes quite firmly; if the pots are in a straight line, the canes in their turn can be tied to a wire running along the row from a post at either end. This will prevent them from blowing over. Buy some No-Soil compost and sow winter-flowering stock seed. A few days later, sow primula seed for summer flowering. Pot-grown lilies may need a top dressing of No-Soil compost. The seedling cinerarias may be potted on into 7.5-cm (3-in) pots, and the earlier struck cuttings of poinsettias can also go into small pots.

Seedlings of the scented humea elegans should be pricked out, and gloriosa seedlings and thunia and centradenia cuttings potted up. Continue to water carefully, only using the watering can when the plants actually need moisture. Remember that as a rule more plants are ruined more by over-watering than under-watering. If there is a dull sound when you tap the pots there is plenty of moisture present, but if you hear a clear ring the pots are dry.

July

First weekend

General   The principal task this month is keeping the plants free from pests and diseases – which is where organic insecticides like derris and pyrethrum come in. For fungus diseases, use karathane in the case of mildews, and colloidal sulphur for scab on apples and pears and black spot on roses.

This is also the month for gathering herbs and drying them for the winter.

Lawns   In dry weather, continue to water your lawn. It pays to feed it at the same time. You can buy an adaptor to connect to your hose, so that liquid manure in the right proportions is taken in and applied through the sprinkler.

Flowers   Bearded irises are best divided in the first week of July. Plant the rhizomes shallowly, for they like sun. Fork in bonemeal at 100–125 g to the square metre (4–5 oz to the square yard) before replanting. If you have been troubled with root rot in the past, it pays to water the ground thoroughly with a 2 per cent solution of formaldehyde first, and then to cover the ground with some sacks soaked in the same solution. Leave the sacks on for a week, then fork the ground over to get rid of the fumes before planting up.

Sow hollyhock seed to raise new plants. Raise some East Lothian stocks in the same way.

Fruit   Cut out all the dead wood that you can see on the cherry trees before the middle of July. Burn all dead wood immediately, and save the ashes to sprinkle along the rows of gooseberries, which appreciate an extra dose of potash. Apricots, peaches and nectarines, especially those growing against walls, need regular soaking with water.

Lorette summer pruning of both apples and pears should be continued, and the fruit thinned if the crop is especially heavy. Most of the pears should be thinned in early July to about 12 cm (5 in) apart. It is better to do this with scissors than with fingers and thumb. Do not, however, try to thin Conference pears. Cooking varieties of plums should be thinned as soon as they are big enough to use. If there is an extra heavy crop of plums, tie up the branches to posts to prevent them breaking.

Vegetables Stump-rooted carrots can be put in this weekend, and so can a good round beet like Boltardy, which should be ready in the autumn or early winter. Sow some turnips at this time of the year. Northerners can now prepare a fine seedbed by forking in sedge peat at one bucketful to the square metre (yard), plus 75 g (3 oz) of fish manure and 75 g (3 oz) of lime. Then the spring cabbage seed should be sown – choose an early cutting type like Primata. If you live in the south, delay this sowing for about 10 days.

For a late crop of French beans, make a final sowing now. If you live in the north, cover them with cloches or frames about the end of September. Earth up the roots of artichokes now if you want a crop of big tubers. Most people allow them to grow as they please, and then are disappointed with the results. Feed the globe artichokes with fish manure at the rate of 75–100 g per square metre (3–4 oz per yard) run.

Flood the celery trenches and use the overhead sprinkler for celeriac – both these crops are likely to suffer from drought this month. There are still many types of winter greens to be planted out, so put them in as soon as there is some land spare after the harvesting of another crop. Take the usual precautions of putting plenty of water into the holes at planting time if the weather is dry; try diluted garlic oil instead if club root has caused trouble in the past.

Greenhouse There is still a good deal of potting-on work to do. Browallias can go into 17- or 20-cm (7- or 8-in) pots, and the begonia Gloire de Lorraine into 15-cm (6-in) pots. Make sure that you have some spare 15-cm (6-in) pots, for later on you will need them for poinsettias. 15-cm (3-in) pots will be needed for primula kewensis, while winter-flowering wallflowers go into the 15-cm (6-in) size. Streptocarpus can go into the same-sized pots, but the primulus obconica, malacoides and sinensis need only grow in 7.5-cm (3-in) pots. It is a good general rule to use No-Soil potting compost for the 7.5-

cm (3-in) pots, and a similar compost for the 15-cm (6-in) pots. The pots, of course, should be well washed first and you should take care to crock them properly. Plastic pots are best.

Second weekend

General This is a very busy month on the whole, with brassicas to sow and plant, the summer pruning to continue and so on. You may have to carry over some of the jobs to next week. You can sow perennials and biennials, while spring-flowering bulbs, whose leaves have now died down, should be lifted carefully for storing. If the many annuals that are flowering now are to continue to look good they must be prevented from seeding, and so flowering heads should be removed when the petals fall.

Go over paths with a strong hormone weedkiller.

Lawns Use a hormone weedkiller on lawns, but be very careful that none of the spray drifts on to the flowers and vegetables.

Flowers The wallflowers that were sown in special beds should now be big enough to transplant into rows 27 cm (9 in) apart, with the plants 15cm (6 in) apart in the rows.

Roses that have had black spot must now be sprayed with colloidal sulphur. Mulch the ground with fresh sedge peat to prevent the spores blowing up from the soil. Apply the mulch 2.5 cm (1 in) deep. There will be some budding of roses to do for those who like to raise their own bushes. Disbud the roses if you want good-sized blooms, rather than quantity. Use a derris-pyrethrum wash as described earlier, if your roses are covered with aphids.

Shrubs and hedges Hedges will need cutting now.

Fruit This is the great month for propagating runners from strawberries. If new beds can be made in July, plants always crop far better in succeeding years than they do from runners planted in September. Help the runners to strike by pegging them and putting sedge peat between the rows. Another trick is to push little wires like hairpins over the runners, immediately behind the tiny plants as they form; in this way you can help them to root. Don't believe gardeners who say you can only take two or three runners from a plant. A hundred runners can be taken from a perfectly healthy specimen of Cambridge

Favourite (Elite strain). You cannot, of course, take that number in July. The best plants are obtained from the runners of one-year-old plants only. These should be kept virus-free.

The raspberry beetle also attacks blackberries, and causes maggoty fruits. As blackberries usually flower late, you should spray in July with liquid derris to control this pest.

Vegetables Thin out the salsify, scorzonera and spinach beet. Clear the early cauliflowers, and plant the colewort seedlings in their place. When the early peas are cleared, plant seedlings of Buttercrunch cos lettuce in their place. Apply a good fish manure along the French bean rows. The onions will probably need a good hoeing, and a little hand weeding. When hoeing onions, always hoe away from them. Take care not to bruise them with the hoe, as this causes them to go to seed before they should.

Keep a sharp eye on potatoes, because this is the time of the year when potato blight starts to make its appearance, spreading gradually from the south to the north. Control by spraying with Bordeaux mixture or, if you live in a smoky district, with Burgundy mixture, giving another application in two or three weeks' time. Alternatively, a copper-lime dust may be used. If a bad attack occurs, cut the haulms off when they die down so as to prevent the tubers from being attacked by the blight spores when they are harvested.

It should be possible to plant another batch of leeks (*plate 5*). The plants that were put in late in June should now be given a feed of diluted liquid manure. It pays to keep leeks growing. When the shallots stop growing and the tops start to die down, it is time to lift them. Dry the bulbs off well, and then store them. Northerners who fear an early frost will probably be pinching out the tops of their tomatoes at about the third truss; the exceptions, of course, are those growing under tall cloches or Access frames.

Lettuces are essential for summer salads. Make another sowing of both the cos and cabbage varieties.

Greenhouse The pelargoniums and ixoras can be propagated by cuttings taken now. Once the arum rhizomes have been cleaned and dried off they can be potted up again in compost. Carefully cut out any sign of bacillus rot, and dip the affected parts in a 2 per cent solution of formaldehyde.

Stake the plants of begonia Gloire de Lorraine, which were potted on last week and which should be growing well. If you are growing peaches under glass continue the pruning and tying in. Tomatoes and cucumbers will have to be looked over again and trained and tied in where necessary. Chrysanthemums will have to be treated in a similar manner. Don't forget to sow winter-flowering stock seeds.

Third weekend

General   Order colchicums and autumn-flowering crocuses, which have to be planted this month if they are going to develop their flowers and produce them in October. It is time now for rose budding, carnation layering and the propagation of shrubs by cuttings. This is the weekend, too, for sowing seed for many of the pot plants, like cinerarias and primulas, for winter decoration indoors.

Start a compost heap, for there is usually plenty of vegetable waste available at this time. For every 15-cm (6-in) thickness of vegetable matter on the heap, sprinkle with a fish or a seaweed fertilizer at 75 g to the square metre (3 oz to the square yard).

Flowers   You can take cuttings of cistus now, and make and insert cuttings of aubrietia and violas. There may be some rooted cuttings of alpines to pot up. Take a look at the rock garden. There will probably be some forking and weeding to carry out in the pockets. Take care of the dahlias by giving them a good watering and a mulching with sedge peat to the depth of 2.5 cm (1 in). Pyrethrum and polyanthuses can be split and replanted.

If the delphiniums have finished flowering, cut them down to within 15 cm (6 in) of soil level, and hoe around and among the plants lightly. Plant some early-flowering chrysanthemums in the herbaceous border, to fill up the gaps.

Shrubs and hedges   If the forsythia is overgrowing, and so proving a nuisance, tie it in rather than cutting back the branches which will, of course, flower in the spring.

Fruit   Cut away the old raspberry canes as soon as they have finished fruiting. At the same time thin out the new canes to about 6 per stool. If the season is hot and sunny, it may be better to leave the cutting out and thinning out until the late autumn. It pays with

A

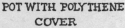

POT WITH POLYTHENE
COVER

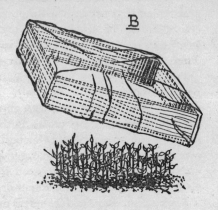

B

BOX SIDES COVERED WITH
POLYTHENE MAKES SIMPLE FRAME

Summer cuttings: (A) in a pot, and (B) in a box covered by a simple frame

loganberries to cut away the old wood immediately after fruiting, whatever the season is like.

Trees growing against walls and fences must be trained. Tie in the growths which will be needed for cropping next year; laterals that are not required can be rubbed out between the thumb and forefinger. Watch out carefully for caterpillars on espaliers, cordons and other types of trees, and spray with a liquid derris immediately you see them.

When the three-year-old strawberry plants have finished cropping, the best thing to do is to dig them into the ground as manure, after sprinkling them with fish manure. It is sometimes possible to get a good crop the fourth year, but usually they deteriorate rapidly after the third. Use the ground for a crop like spring cabbage, followed, say, by early potatoes next year. You can then use that specific piece of ground for strawberries again, and plant them early in August.

Vegetables Start planting some Brussels sprouts, choosing such a variety as Stabilo. Plant out cauliflowers after the early potatoes, which most gardeners will be lifting. If you live in the south, put in a row or two of late runner beans; one of the best varieties for this time of year is Kelvedon Marvel. The rows should be 1.8 metres (6 ft) apart. The Batavian endive is particularly delicious, and this and other types of endive can be sown now. The Batavian endive grows very large, so sow the seed in rows not less than 45 cm (18 in) apart. Thin out the plants to 30 cm (12 in) apart about a month later.

Put in canes 1.5 metres (5 ft) apart, with string stretched in between, to prevent the tall feathery growths of asparagus from flopping over. After the asparagus has been staked, look over sweet corn and aubergines, for the wind may be causing them damage, and stake where necessary. Broad beans can be cleared now; in their place plant a late cabbage like Christmas Drumhead.

Greenhouse Sow freesia seeds thinly in No-Soil seed compost, and when the plants are through, thin them out leaving only seven of them per 12-cm (5-in) pot. Keep the plants in the greenhouse and they will flower next spring. Either this weekend or next, take cuttings of mesembryanthemums, hydrangeas and abutilons. At the same time layer the lapagerias. They usually take about two years before they root properly. Spray pot roses with karathane if they are showing any signs of mildew. Stand hydrangeas out in the sun, in a sheltered place, when they have finished blooming.

Spray chrysanthemums with nicotine to prevent attack by capsids and aphids. You can continue washing the thick rhizomes or roots of the arums in the 2 per cent solution of formaldehyde if you did not finish it last week. Asparagus sprengeri seedlings can be potted on into 7.5-cm (3-in) pots. Sow the seed of herbaceous calceolarias, for when they have grown you will be able to keep them in a cool house. Other sowings you can make are those of primula malacoides and the nierembergias. Plant out Malmaison carnations so that they can be layered in the frames.

Fourth weekend
Flowers Flag irises that have leaf spot can be sprayed with colloidal sulphur. Many perennials can be sown at this time of year. Border carnations can be layered. Bulbs that have been growing can be lifted and dried off and, provided they are stored in a frostproof place, can be used again next year for spring bedding. Autumn crocuses can be planted, and so may colchicums and erythroniums.

Take cuttings of veronicas and nepeta. If you like subtropical bedding, plant it about this time. Peonies may have quite a few dead flowerheads on them – cut these off. Cut back also the roses that have finished flowering. Sweet peas will appreciate a feed of fish manure at 75 g (3 oz) to the yard run. Feed the roses at the same time, and at a similar rate.

Keep cutting off the heads of the bedding violas as they die, to prevent them from going to seed (once they do this, they cease to flower). The easiest way to propagate anchusas is to take root cuttings now. Rambler roses need pruning as they cease to flower, the only exceptions being those to be used for cuttings.

Shrubs and hedges Beech and privet hedges need to be cut.

Fruit If you want to try budding, this is the right time of year, provided suitable stocks are used. If scab is a nuisance on pears, spray with colloidal sulphur.

The morello cherries will be ready for picking. Blackcurrants should also be ready, but check them carefully for they are inclined to look black and ripe before they really are. The advantage in having several varieties is that you can spread the picking season over two or three weeks.

Vegetables Top-dress frame cucumbers, as advised for greenhouse cucumbers. Swedes should be sown now – choose a variety like Tipperary. Always take precautions against club root in swedes. Draw the outer leaves of the cos lettuce together by putting rubber bands over them. In this way they produce good hearts. Raffia will do the job just as well, but the operation takes longer.

Seeds of the red cabbage Ruby Ball can be sown. Savoys such as Ormskirk Late should be planted up, and carefully watered in. The earlier-sown carrots and turnips will need thinning, and the sooner this is done the better. Be sure to firm along the row of carrots afterwards.

The mint bed should be hand-weeded, but you can hoe the rest of the herb border. Celery will also need hoeing and spraying with a nicotine wash to prevent celery fly laying their eggs. Pickling onions should be lifted and dried off. Continue to pick peas, for the more you pick them the better the crop. Potatoes should be earthed up as needed, and a late batch of broccoli planted out. A row of curly kales should also be planted.

August

First weekend

General Never be satisfied with your garden. This is an extremely good time of the year to go round with a pencil and paper and make some notes on what you like and what you don't like about it. Then you can plan for next year, and make any necessary changes.

Order bulbs for Christmas flowering. 'Prepared' (cooled) bulbs are a little more expensive, but will flower sooner. Pot up the bulbs in sedge peat or fibre, or even in soil, and place them in the dark for at least nine weeks before they are brought into the light.

Flowers Order autumn bulbs, if you haven't already done so.

Shrubs and hedges If you want to plant evergreens in the early autumn send in the order now, so that the shrubs will arrive at the right time.

Fruit There should be a number of apples to pick soon, including the varieties Irish Peach and Beauty of Bath, Lady Sudeley, Tydeman's Early Worcester, Laxton's Advance and Scarlet Pimpernel. The last-mentioned variety, many gardeners think, has definitely supplanted Beauty of Bath. If your early apples have a tendency to drop before they are picked, spray the trees with a special hormone solution to make the fruit remain tightly attached to the spurs for two or three weeks longer. When spraying, be sure to soak the stalks of the apples thoroughly, for these are the important part.

The earliest varieties of pears may be ripening, especially if they are growing on walls. The wasps will be interested in them, and it pays to pop a small thin paper bag over the spurs, to prevent the birds from pecking the fruits, and the wasps from attacking them. As brown rot disease inevitably enters through a wound, it is most important to keep the skin on the pears unblemished.

Vegetables Thin the earlier-sown carrots, and eat the thinnings. Take the necessary precautions against the ravages of carrot fly maggot by applying naphthaline dust in between the rows at 25 g to the metre (1 oz to the yard) run. Thin down turnips and parsnips to 20 cm (8 in) apart. Watch out for flea beetle on the turnips and, if the leaves are pitted, dust immediately with plenty of derris.

Corn salad is a very delicious winter crop, especially the variety Regence. Sow it in rows 30 cm (1 ft) apart, and in drills 1 cm ($\frac{1}{2}$ in) deep, on a warm south border. When they come through, thin out the plants to 20 cm (8 in) apart.

Sow onions this weekend, choosing a variety like White Lisbon; so that you have plenty of salad onions later on. Make the rows 30cm (1 ft) apart on some finely prepared firm ground. If you live in the south make a second sowing of spring cabbage on a seedbed enriched with sedge peat applied at one bucketful to the square metre (yard). The idea is to raise plants that you can put out into the open about 15 September.

Greenhouse Transfer zonal pelargoniums to cold frames this weekend, cutting them back hard at the same time. The moment the young shoots start to develop, use them as cuttings. Adopt a similar system with regal pelargoniums. Large specimens in pots must be deflowered; remove the blossoms weekend by weekend until, say, early November. There will then be plenty of flowers in the winter.

Second weekend
General If you are going away on holiday any time from this weekend onwards, cut back most of the flowers quite hard, so that when you return the garden will be a blaze of colour again instead of a mass of dying plants or browning seed pods. If possible, make some arrangements with a neighbour to water the plants in the greenhouse, and do the same for him or her in return.

Cut lavender for drying. It is always better to remove the flower heads while they are still at their best. If you do not cut the flowers regularly, the plants tend to grow straggly.

Flowers Divide and transplant amaryllis and hippeastrum, both of which like to grow in a really well-drained warm position. If you have a nice sunny wall, then plant these at its base and you will be delighted with the results.

1 The pink blossom stage of apples when the main spraying with a fungicide is done

2 The lilac-mauve autumn crocus, *Colchicum autumnale*, grows to only six inches. It is sometimes called 'naked lady' because it has no leaves when it flowers

3 Applying mixed cement to form a path
4 Levelling concrete carefully with a wooden leveller to make a wide path

5 Planting leeks with a dibber. Note the depth at which the dibber is put in

6 Station sowing in a seedbed

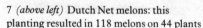

7 *(above left)* Dutch Net melons: this planting resulted in 118 melons on 44 plants

8 Chrysanthemum leaves showing leaf miner damage: plants afflicted with this should be sprayed with Malathion, and the greenhouse in which they grow should be fumigated

9 *(above right)* Using a flame gun for burning weeds

10 *(below right)* This kind of oscillating lawn sprinkler offers a choice of four watering patterns and covers up to 1800 sq ft of lawn

11 Applying lawn feed with a mechanical spreader

12 Making a twist of straw at the top of a clamp of potatoes for aeration

13 This cedar greenhouse gives the maximum of light

14 Blanching is assisted if straw is put in between self-blanching celery

15 Suttons Little Gem, a lettuce which is an intermediate type between cabbage lettuce and the true cos, is dwarf, compact, crisp, medium green in colour with few outside leaves

16 Leek Catalina, one of the Dobies varieties

Disbud the chrysanthemums in earnest this weekend if you want large blooms. Leave the end flower bud on each growth and remove the side ones. Feed the dahlias with a liquid manure, which can be bought in bottles with full instructions. Remember that this will cause the plants to flower well, and also to produce better tubers for next season. If the weather is dry don't be afraid to use plenty of water – overhead sprinklers are ideal for this purpose: attach them to a hose and leave them in the same position for about three-quarters of an hour, so that the ground gets a thorough soaking.

Fruit This is an excellent weekend for planting strawberries. Plant them in soil that is thoroughly enriched with organic matter. Prune blackcurrants, after picking all the fruit, by cutting out the old wood and reducing in length the branches that are drooping towards the ground. Watch out for American mildew on gooseberries and spray with Karathane.

Look at the plums and pick any that are ripe. Continue to pick them as they become ripe. Look also at the early peaches, and start picking them. Some of the later varieties are probably being damaged by wasps, so protect them with bags as described for pears last weekend. There may be some Brown Turkey figs ready to pick this weekend; they need gathering when they are soft and ready to use.

Vegetables Sow the main batch of winter spinach, using one of the prickly-seeded varieties. Soak the seeds overnight before sowing. Also sow a bulbing onion such as Unwin's Reliance. Thin out the plants in the spring to about 10 cm (4 in) apart and you will have a very good crop.

Bend over the tops of the early bulbing onions (as the result of sowing last August) to help ripen them. If possible, use the back of a wooden rake for this. Then leave the rows for a fortnight and you should be able to fork up the bulbs and gradually dry them off, laying them on their sides. So this weekend you start off your next year's onions, and begin to ripen off last year's onions sown at this time.

Greenhouse Sow Persian cyclamen seed this weekend, in No-Soil seed compost. Space out the seed as near 1 cm ($\frac{1}{2}$ in) apart as possible, and cover it afterwards with a little silver sand. Put a sheet of glass over the top and a piece of newspaper over this; stand the box on the staging of the greenhouse at a temperature of 13–15°C (55–60°F). If you are growing stocks it may be necessary to give the seedlings a top dressing of No-Soil potting compost to a depth of 3 mm (⅛ in) or so. If you are growing centradenias, pot them on from 7.5-cm (3-in) pots to 15-cm (6-in) pots full of No-Soil compost. It may be necessary to pot on cinerarias and primulas, such as malacoides and stellata, at the same time.

The interesting thing about coleus cuttings is that they may be nodal (i.e. cuts made at a node or joint) or internodal (i.e. with the cuts made anywhere in between nodes or joints). This makes striking cuttings very simple. Use a mixture of sedge peat and coarse silver sand, and do make sure that it is river sand and not seashore sand.

Also strike cuttings of various species of begonias, calceolarias, heliotropes ('cherry pie') and verbena. Nodal cuttings must be taken for all these.

Freesias are very popular, and if bulbs are bought they should be potted up in a mixture of sedge peat and soil into the 15-cm (6-in) pots in which flowering is to take place. The achimenes, which have recently flowered, will have to be dried off gradually in a cold frame before sowing.

Third weekend

General   Keep a sharp look out for insect pests which can be very troublesome at this time of year. Watch out for potato blight, too, as this will not only attack the rows of maincrops but will also drift on to the outdoor tomatoes as well. Bordeaux dust is the simplest method of control.

Mulchings are tremendously important this month, and readers who have not used sedge peat 2.5 cm (1 in) deep all over the ground in May or early June – the ideal method – should now use lawn mowings as a mulch or even lay thick brown paper on the soil in between the rows of vegetable plants. The difficulty about paper mulching is that the paper has to be prevented from blowing away, with little mounds of soil. It is also possible to mulch with three- or four-year-old sawdust – but fresh sawdust is no good, for it has a serious de-nitrifying effect on the soil.

Flowers   Cut down to within 15 cm (6 in) of soil level all the plants that have finished flowering in the last week or two. Feed the rose-beds with a fish fertilizer at 75–100 g to the square metre (3–4 oz to the square yard). Hoe this in lightly afterwards and, if the weather is very dry, add water. Look for suckers that may be growing up from the roots of hybrid tea roses, and cut these off right down to their base. Plant out in a sheltered spot the Brompton stocks that are to flower early next year; put them in about 30 cm (1 ft) square.

This is a good weekend to take geranium cuttings. There is no need to use a frame or greenhouse – the cuttings will take quite well in sandy soil out of doors. Make the cuts with a sharp knife or razor blade just below a node, remove the bottom one or two leaves and dibble the cuttings in so that they are nice and firm, 7.5 cm (3 in) or so deep.

If you want to have better blooms on your michaelmas daisies, go over the plants this weekend and reduce the number of shoots coming up from the stools.

Check over the winter bedding plants, such as wallflowers and forget-me-nots, and if you do not think they are growing fast enough, apply some dried blood along the rows at 25 g to the metre (1 oz to the yard) run and, if the soil is dry, water this in.

Fruit The moment all the dessert gooseberries have been picked, and this may happen at the weekend, cut back the drooping branches to keep them off the soil, making certain that the cuts are made just above a bud. At the same time, look out for suckers coming up from the roots. Cut these back below the soil – preferably right to their base. In the case of raspberries, it is quite a good idea to cut away the canes that have recently fruited to within 2.5 cm (1 in) of soil level, and then to tie in the new young canes in their place. This gives the young wood the chance of ripening so that it will crop well next season.

Start to do your summer pruning on peaches and nectarines, the idea being to remove the shoots that will not be required next season. Treat apricot trees in a similar manner; remember that it is no use keeping the very strong young wood, for this will not flower. Once all the fruit has been picked from the wall trees, it is quite a good plan to spray the leaves and branches with plenty of clean water. Give the borders a good flooding also, to encourage the trees to build up for next year's cropping.

Vegetables Lift the spring-sown beetroot; those not required immediately should be put into a heap and covered with some soil. This prevents the roots from shrivelling and allows them to be used as required. Early carrots should be treated in the same way, for otherwise they may start to split.

For an early crop of lettuce, sow a variety like All the Year Round or Hilde this weekend and allow it to winter out of doors. Sow them in rows 30 cm (1 ft) apart, thinning the seedlings to 20 cm (8 in) apart in the spring. Thin out Batavian endive to about 30 cm (12 in) apart.

Dig some of the second early potatoes; if there are none, some of the early maincrops may be ready. If you have been unable to spray against potato blight, and the tops are brown, cut them down to soil level before lifting the tubers in order to prevent their being infected. Attend to the outdoor tomatoes, pinch out the main growing point on the tops of the plants when the fourth truss is formed, and remove all the side shoots regularly. Those who live in the north may only be able to grow three trusses, and so should stop the plants accordingly.

Greenhouse The leaf miner is apt to rear its head at this time of year to attack many different plants, especially cinerarias and chrysanthemums (*plate* 7). Buy a suitable smoke and fumigate the greenhouse. Keep tying in the chrysanthemums as they need it, and do some disbudding this weekend. Stopping, and the taking or pinching of crown buds, should be done now.

Fourth weekend
General Bulbs should now be planted for bowl and pot culture. It is also a good time for gathering seeds of flowering plants. You cannot always guarantee good results from your own seeds, but it is always interesting to try. You only have to leave on a few seeding pods to get an ample supply – remember that to allow plants to seed indiscriminately causes unnecessary strain on their development.

Use weedkiller on the garden paths again.

Lawns Give the lawn a good mowing and follow this by a light rolling, unless, of course, it happens to be a wet period. Only mow when the lawn is dry.

Flowers Attend to staking and tying in the herbaceous border –

September is often a windy month. Arum lilies, planted out in the open for growing on, should be divided and potted up into 17- or 20-cm (7- or 8-in) pots ready for bringing in to the greenhouse early in October. The eremurus, or foxtail lily, is one of the most beautiful plants to have in the flower border. Now is the time to carry out the division of the older specimens, but do it carefully because the roots are brittle.

You will have no difficulty in propagating sedums, saxifrages and sempervivums this weekend by inserting rosettes or cuttings in sandy soil in a frame. This is also a good time of year for taking cuttings of fuchsias, verbenas, hydrangeas and petunias.

Fruit   Strawberry runners should be removed. The earliest and best of them will have produced roots, and these should now be planted out into the bed where they will crop next year. Any runners not required should be cut off just the same and put on the compost heap. In the case of older rows of strawberries, remove any of the leaves that are brown or diseased, and give the plants a good soaking with a derris wash. Dissolve 25 g (1 oz) of liquid derris in a 12-litre (2-gal) bucket of water, and add a dessertspoonful of liquid detergent. Fork lightly into the rows of strawberries after this work has been done. If you have used straw to keep the berries clean, rake it off and put it on the compost heap to form manure; if sedge peat has been used, leave it there. When hoeing afterwards, draw the soil up to the plants rather than away from them, for new roots are formed higher up the crown each season. But if the soil is mulched with sedge peat, do not hoe.

Some plum pruning can be done, especially in gardens where silver leaf is troublesome. It is better to prune now and not get the disease, than to prune in the winter and suffer from it.

Vegetables   Cut vegetable marrows and outdoor cucumbers before they get too old and hard. Gather summer squashes as they become ready. Sow one or two short rows of a good red pickling cabbage like Niggerhead; the idea is to raise good plants for putting out in their permanent cropping position next spring. Sow parsley in a sheltered place. To ensure success give the soil a good dusting with lime afterwards. Go over the rows of seakale spinach and spinach beet, and cut off old leaves and stems.

The earliest celery should need its first earthing up this weekend.

First fork the soil along the rows to provide some fine earth, then grip the stems of the plants before drawing up the soil to them. If you are growing runner beans on the flat, spaced out at 90 cm (3 ft) apart, cut them back this weekend with a pair of shears. If you are growing beans up poles or wire netting give the rows a good mulching with lawn mowings or sedge peat, and syringe the plants thoroughly in the evening.

Greenhouse If you want to force some Cambridge Favourite Elite strawberries in pots for the winter, pot up some of the best plants struck in the earlier part of the month into 15-cm (6-in) pots filled with No-Soil potting compost. Plant so that the crowns are towards one side of the pot, and then the developed fruit will hang over the pot naturally.

Carry out some propagation of succulents or cacti. Allow the cut part to dry a little before attempting to insert it into sand. Pot on the two-year-old cyclamens into their 15-cm (6-in) pots, using the No-Soil potting compost. Put the pots on the staging of the greenhouse at a temperature of 19°C (65°F). The melons should be starting to ripen this weekend, so keep the greenhouse airy and warm and reduce the amount of water given to the borders.

September

There will be many apples and pears to pick, although some of the varieties will be left until October. Bulbs can still be put in bowls and pots this month. Evergreens can be planted, and many shrub plants can be increased by means of cuttings, for this is a great propagating month also. It is a good time for sowing a new lawn, so make sure of a good strain of grass by writing to a reputable nursery straight away.

First weekend
Flowers Violets can be planted out into frames this month, using No-Soil compost. Make certain the compost in the frames is parallel to the glass light above, and that the plants themselves are not too far away from the glass. Plant firmly and leave the frames open until frost occurs, when the glass should go over. Prevent red spider by syringeing the undersides of the violet leaves. Plant some more alpines, so that they will become established before the hard weather sets in.

Make use of your cold frame by taking cuttings of violas, marguerites, nepetas, pentstemons and calceolarias. Take cuttings of antirrhinums, though this is not really necessary since it is possible to buy seeds of varieties free from rust. Use No-Soil compost, cover it with 1 cm (½ in) of silver sand before the cuttings are inserted, and water through a fine rose. Be sure to dibble in firmly. Give your cuttings some shade for about a week, and spray twice a day, in the morning and late afternoon. Plenty of ventilation should be given once the cuttings have rooted. Be sure to close the lights tightly whenever there is any risk of frost, covering them with matting to give extra protection.

Fruit Apples and pears should be picked as soon as they are ready. You can tell when they are ripe because they come away cleanly from the spurs when lifted slightly with the hands. Be careful not to grip the fruit with your fingers, or they will bruise. If pears are mealy, they have been left on the trees too long. The early and mid-season varieties must always be picked before the green base colour has turned yellow. The majority of pears will have been picked by next weekend.

There may be some plums ripe enough to pick, especially Jefferson's Gage and the old Transparent Gage.

Vegetables The Ailsa Craig and Reliance onion should be sown early this month. The rows must be 30 cm (12 in) apart if you want to grow big specimens; do not thin until the spring. Keep the rows clean and free from weeds before winter sets in. Prepare a very fine seedbed by forking in a little sedge peat and raking thoroughly until the particles of soil are as fine as grains of wheat. If the seedbed is large enough, make another sowing of a quick-growing carrot, to pull the young roots in the winter. Thin out the turnips sown in August so that the leaves of one plant cannot touch the leaves of the next. Continue to earth up your celery, to have it ready by mid-October.

Start to harvest maincrop potatoes. Dry the tubers in the sun for a few hours after lifting; the skin will then set before the tubers are moved. This makes a great deal of difference to the keeping qualities of the tubers. The little potatoes, known as chats, should be used straight away. If the potato tops were attacked by potato blight, cut off all the tops before attempting to dig up the roots. The spores will then be prevented from dropping on to the tubers as they are lifted, which would infect the potatoes themselves. It is quite all right to put the tops on the compost heap, provided they are sprinkled with an activator to make them rot down quickly.

Greenhouse Keep potting up your bulbs as you buy them. In this way they will be ready for forcing in about eight weeks' time. They must be in the dark for that period. Bulbs do better if the pots are left outside on a path or concrete yard, covered with sand or ashes, than if they are put in a cupboard in the house. If you only have a cupboard, the bulbs will have to be watered from time to time.

Another potting up job is that of the rooted cuttings of pelargoniums. They should be planted one to a pot. Carnations also should be potted on from 7.5-cm (3-in) pots to 15-cm (6-in) pots, and the Malmaison types should be staked. Continue to disbud chrysanthemums and tie them up also. Take cuttings of fuchsias. Re-pot the cyclamen that were raised from seed sown the previous year.

Second weekend

General As the evenings begin to shorten many people do less gardening especially those who arrive home late. It is, however, very important to keep on hoeing. Remember that this will save you time and effort in the long run. A tremendous number of weeds seed at this time of year, so continue to hoe shallowly, or you will have weed problems in the spring.

Flowers Plant daffodils and almost any other bulbs except tulips. Make quite certain that the bulbs saved from last year are firm and healthy. Any soft or diseased specimens should be burned at once. Look out for ink disease spots on iris reticulata. If there are few spots, remove the diseased portions but, if they are badly covered, burn the bulbs.

Plant out Brompton stocks in a sheltered place, to flower early in the spring. Crown imperials may be put in now. Schizostylus may be planted also, or if they are in already, divide the plants and replant. Sow sweet peas now (and cover them with cloches from the middle of October onwards).

Pink cuttings should have rooted well by now, and they can be planted firmly in the places where they are to flower. Certain annuals, such as cornflower, calendula, larkspur and candytuft, will live through the winter if the seeds can be sown now. If you want them for cut flowers, the rows should be 30 cm (1 ft) apart, but if they are for an early show in flower border sow the seeds in drifts or patches. Later thin the plants out to about 30 cm (1 ft) apart in the case of the taller kinds, and 15 cm (6 in) apart with the dwarfer ones. It is best to do this before the winter sets in.

Fruit Apples and pears should be stored separately. Use paper wraps for those you are going to store for a long time, because this helps to keep the flavour. Pears need a storage temperature of 5–7°C (40–45°F). Store them in trays if possible, and don't let the fruits touch each other. A good succession of pears would be Durondeau (October), Doyenne de Comice (October), Charles Ernest (November), Fondante de Thirriot (December) and Josephine de Malines (January).

The damsons should be ready for picking, although Merryweather, which is a late variety, must wait until the end of the month. Both Coe's Golden Drop Plum and Kirke's Blue plum should be ready this weekend. Later on in the month the Giant Prune, Pond's Seedling and Reine Claude de Bavay will be ready.

Vegetables Cut back the tops of late peas by 2.5–5 cm (1–2 in) with shears; the pods will swell better as a result. Carry on earthing up your celery by gripping the stems tightly and then drawing the soil up to them. In this way, the soil is prevented from getting into the hearts, and slugs' eggs and baby slugs are kept out. Have a look at spring-sown onions during this weekend; they will possibly be ready for harvesting. Root crops also need attention for, with the beginning of the autumn rain, they may start into growth again, and splitting takes place.

Greenhouse Plant out sweet violets in frames, ready for winter flowering. Sow the seed of antirrhinums in No-Soil compost both for bedding and to produce plants for potting up. Pot on the lilium longiflorum for early flowering, then put the plants into the cold frame for the time being. If solanums and bouvardias have been planted out, lift them and pot them up for the winter. November-flowering chrysanthemums will be lifted to bring in in October; cut the soil now with a spade for 15 cm (6 in) around each plant; this promotes good root growth which can easily be lifted with a good ball of soil in a week or two.

Third weekend

General Remember what I said earlier about picking apples and pears – they must be gathered as soon as they part readily from the spurs on the branches. If they are allowed to fall on the ground they bruise, and then they cannot be stored successfully, for bruises invariably let in brown rot disease.

Lawns This is a good weekend for sowing a lawn, but it is worthwhile getting the correct pedigree seed from a reliable seedsman. Young grass invariably suffers from a summer drought when it has been sown in the autumn, so it will need watering well.

Mow and edge existing lawns until about the end of the month.

Flowers Any climbing roses that are making prolific growth should be pruned. Again, look for rose suckers and cut them off at the roots.

The annuals sown in the spring will by now have finished flowering and will have to be cleared away. Put them on the compost heap, together with any other waste vegetable matter, and sprinkle them with an activator such as fish manure. Make sure that the michaelmas daisies, chrysanthemums and dahlias are all firmly tied. If you tie newspaper over dahlias on frosty nights you will be able to prolong their flowering season. Keep your eyes open and take precautions if you think there is going to be a frost.

Plant out your polyanthuses where they are going to flower. Continue disbudding chrysanthemums and michaelmas daisies if you want bigger blooms. Remove the flower heads as they finish to prevent them seeding, and you can prolong the flowering season.

Shrubs and hedges Prune back clematis and wisteria. It is very important to tie in all the growths carefully before autumn and winter winds start to blow.

Fruit Examine the budded stocks of young fruit trees and loosen the ties. Mark the trees and bushes which you think will be of no further use, and then in the winter you will be able to grub them up. Make certain that all is ready in the fruit store. The walls may need to be whitewashed and the woodwork scrubbed with a 2 per cent solution of formaldehyde in water. Air the store well after this treatment to disperse the fumes. Early apples and pears should be taken into the house to be used straight away, for they will not keep.

If you want to plant new fruit bushes in October and early November, send in your order straight away. Take care to include all the necessary pollinators or you will be disappointed. Go round filberts and cobnut trees and cut away any suckers that are growing up; trace these down to their base and sever them there. Pick mulberries. Cut down the old fruiting canes of the loganberries and blackberries, and tie in the young canes in their places.

Vegetables Frosts have a habit of coming suddenly, so keep an eye on the tomatoes. With outdoor varieties, it is wise to pick off the green trusses and bring them into the house or greenhouse for ripening off. Some of them can be used for ketchup, sauce and chutney, and the others can be ripened off by being cut down and laid on sedge peat underneath cloches or frames, which become very useful at this time of year for protecting plants.

Feed leeks regularly at this time of the year; it makes a surprising amount of difference. Apply a liquid manure, properly diluted, about once a week from now on until the third week of October, provided the weather remains good. A gallon of the diluted solution is sufficient for a 1.75-metre (6-ft) row. Transplant winter lettuces into their frames or under cloches, and force a little mint in the greenhouse by cutting down the tops now, so that the roots will be ready for lifting about the end of October.

Greenhouse Make sure that all the late chrysanthemums in pots are in the greenhouse before the frost comes – and this is sometimes as early as the third week in September. Stake the begonias Gloire de Lorraine, the poinsettias and the pycnostachys. The salvias also may need staking. Primula stellata and primula malacoides will need to be potted on. If you have any deciduous azaleas that are to flower under glass, keep the pots in the frame so that, after they are lifted and potted, they are quite cool.

Sow seed now for schizanthus or butterfly flower, in 7.5-cm (3-in) pots in No-Soil compost. Clarkia can be sown in the same way, to have a good show of these flowers in the spring. The seedlings of humea elegans can be pricked out in No-Soil potting compost. Show pelargoniums should be potted on from 7.5-cm (3-in) pots to 15-cm (6-in) pots. Treat your cinerarias in the same way.

Fourth weekend
Flowers Transplant red hot pokers, delphiniums, nepeta, eryngium, gaillardia and so on. Move pyrethrums into a bed where the soil is well drained, if the plants were split up in July. Those who live in the north should not attempt this late planting. All the tender bedding plants, such as the heliotropes, begonias and cannas will have to be lifted before the end of the month to go under glass.

Shrubs and hedges Send in your order for any shrubs you want, especially the deciduous kinds, which can be planted early in the autumn. Rhododendrons are best moved at this time of the year.

Fruit   The banding material for the grease-bands you must put on your trees early in October should be ordered now. Alternatively you can use a special preparation of vegetable oils which is applied direct to the trunk. The trunks of cherry trees should be sprayed with a white oil before the leaves fall, and plums should be treated in a similar manner. You will then prevent the spores of shot hole fungus dropping from the foliage and infecting the main stems.

Most people like peaches, but comparatively few grow them in their gardens in the open. It is possible to plant peach trees this weekend where they are to fruit. Many bush trees do well, even north of Birmingham, provided they are in sheltered positions. Wasps are a nuisance at this time of year. Find where their nests are and put a handful of derris powder over the holes to get rid of them.

Vegetables   The spring cabbage should by now have been planted out and, if you have not raised your own seedlings, buy them. They should be planted on the 1-ft-square basis though, in a sheltered garden, with a larger variety like Durham Early, the rows should be 45 cm (18 in) apart. Prevent club root by placing a small piece of garlic in the holes at planting time.

If you have no glass available, you may have to put sheets of newspaper over marrows and outdoor cucumbers to protect them on frosty nights. Clear away the old dead leaves of the rhubarb, and the moment that frost has touched the stems, remove them and fork over the ground lightly around the crowns.

Protect late-sown dwarf beans with cloches or frames, and pot up seedling cauliflowers into their 7.5-cm (3-in) pots or soil blocks. Plant out the endive in rows 45 cm (18 in) apart, with at least 30 cm (1 ft) between the plants. Corn salad may be sown in a warm border, and maincrop carrots and beetroot should be stored in clamps or buries.

If you have a dark, warm, well-insulated shed, use this in which to prepare mushroom beds.

Greenhouse   Melons should now be growing in a temperature of about 25°C (75°F). If it is very sunny they may need a good deal of syringing. Continue to syringe even if the fruits are ripening. Peaches should have all the air possible, both night and day. The ventilators can also be opened wide in the case of vines, which should have many of their lateral growths cut away. The heat should be kept on if they are carrying fruit, in order to ripen it properly.

Grow sweet peas under glass in 7.5-cm (3-in) pots. Look out for leaf miners and aphids, as well as other pests on greenhouse plants, and either spray with derris or use a smoke. Before the winter sets in, give the greenhouse glass a good wash over, using a detergent to remove grime on the outside. The green algae which collect between the overlap of the glass can be removed with a very thin palette knife inserted between the panes. Wash the woodwork, too.

October

Planting trees early in the winter allows them to become established before the really cold weather sets in. If they are planted before the end of this month, they grow well.

The leaves are starting to fall from the trees thick and fast, and you will have a job keeping the garden tidy.

First weekend

Flowers   Root cuttings of many plants can be taken in sandy soil in frames. Plants that can be propagated in this way include oriental poppies, yuccas, anemones, gaillardias, anchusas, clerodendrons, eryngiums and statices. If eelworm has been partcularly bad on the phloxes, it is better to propagate them by root cuttings inserted into sandy soil in boxes, which are then put in a cold frame. Ordinary cuttings may be taken of both rambler and briar roses, while gardeners who budded the briars last June should now cut these back to just above a bud.

The removal of summer bedding plants should be completed as soon as possible, to get the spring bedding in position. Siberian and ordinary wallflowers can be planted out now. Cut back, by about a quarter, the longer leaves of the irises and weed the bed thoroughly; cutting back seems to help control leaf spot disease. Spraying with colloidal sulphur, before the beds are lightly forked over, is useful here. The herbaceous borders can be cleaned up by cutting away old stems and forking over the borders lightly. But if the border is mulched with sedge peat 2.5 cm (1 in) deep, leave it alone.

Shrubs and hedges   The various types of berberis species can be cut back now, especially those that have flowered early in the season.

Fruit   There may be nuts to gather this weekend, either filberts or cobnuts. If autumn-fruiting raspberries have been down for more than three years, it is best to replant them.

Complete picking the apples. The following varieties are, as a rule, gathered at this time; Allington Pippin, Barnack Beauty, Blenheim Orange, Charles Ross, Christmas Pearmain, Claygate Pearmain, Cornish Gillyflower, Cox's Orange Pippin, Crimson Cox, Eastern Orange, Edward VII, Golden Noble, Herring's Pippin, Lane's Prince Albert, Laxton's Fortune, Monarch, Rival, Royal Jubilee, St Cecilia, Sunset, The Queen, Upton Pyne and Wealthy.

Vegetables Get as much shallow digging done as possible, and leave the land rough so that the frosts can get at it and break it down. Ridging may be adopted if the soil is particularly heavy. It exposes much more soil to the frost and cold winds and, although it take longer to do, it is worth it. If you are a non-digger, like me, just cover the soil with compost towards the end of the month and let the worms pull it in.

If the onions are ripe enough, as they should be by now, they can be lifted and stored. A good method of keeping the bulbs is to rope them together and hang them under the eaves of the loft. Continue to earth up celery and leeks, making sure that no earth gets between the celery stems. Lift late-planted potatoes, and store them in clamps or buries. The lower leaves of Brussels sprouts will probably be turning yellow, so remove them and put them on the compost heap to rot down for manure. This lets light and air into the plants.

In the south, sow a Trocadero type of lettuce in the open – Unrivalled is a good strain. Those who sowed a late batch of spring cabbage should now have good plants for putting out; a good variety for this is Winnigstadt. Sow lettuces in frames, and prepare the soil now. Hoe any plots of vegetable crops that may be growing.

Greenhouse The bleeding heart or dicentra spectabilis forces quite easily under glass if you use No-Soil potting compost. After potting, put the plants in cold frames for about three weeks. Solomon's seal can be treated in the same manner; it is attractive as a table decoration.

The primula sinensis can be taken from the cold frames, and can go into the greenhouse at a temperature of $13°C$ ($55°F$). Decaying foliage at the base of the chrysanthemums should be removed, and some gardeners dust their plants thoroughly at this time of year with kara-thane dust. You can buy a dust gun for this. During this month dusting is considered more suitable in the greenhouse because, when spraying, the atmosphere tends to be laden with moisture. For leaf miners use a nicotine dust.

Second weekend

General October may be a mild month, but can be just the opposite. Gardeners must take special care and the tenderest plants must be housed. Cannas, begonias and so on must be brought in, but dahlias can be left until they are actually cut by the frost. It is a great gar-dening period, with much planting and transplanting to be done. Herbaceous borders, for instance, can be replanned and renovated. Less water and less air is given under glass.

Flowers The gladiolus primulinus hybrids can be left in the beds if desired, or they can be dug up every other year. Evening primroses, foxgloves, sweet williams and canterbury bells can all be planted. Give them plenty of room and they will do well – do not be tempted to overcrowd them. They will be better if a little fish manure is forked into the ground first. Sedge peat should also be added at the rate of a bucketful to the square metre (yard), and at a slightly higher rate if the soil is sandy or very heavy. The ordinary gladioli corms, especially the grandiflora types, should be lifted for drying.

While renovating herbaceous borders, propagate the peonies by division. One of the best ways to divide clumps of plants is to insert two forks into the clump, back to back, and then lever them apart. The colvillei strains of gladioli can be put in about this weekend. Ixias and sparaxis can also be planted about the same time, provided you put them into a sunny border and preferably in soil which has been raised above the general level. If you didn't plant red hot pokers and eremuri last weekend you should plant them now.

Fruit Take cuttings of gooseberries as early as possible; they always strike better when they are taken just before the leaves fall. The cuttings should be about 30 cm (12 in) long. Leave the top three buds, but remove all the others; then insert the cutting 15 cm (6 in) deep in the ground. If the soil is very heavy, put in a little sand at the bottom on which the cutting can rest. Take cuttings of worcester-berries at the same time, and in the same way.

Put grease-bands on the trees. Those that were put on some time ago should be looked over and any leaves or twigs sticking to them should be removed, for these will form little bridges over which the female winter moths can climb and lay their eggs.

Vegetables Late beetroot and carrots should be lifted now and stored in hales or clamps. Leave them in a heap to 'sweat' for a week, and then cover them with straw and soil. Leave a tight twist of straw poking out at the top to enable the heap to breathe (*plate 12*). Handle the beetroot carefully, or they may bleed. It is best not to knock off all the soil from the roots – store them with some of the earth still clinging to them. Do not store any injured carrots, or fungus disease may set in and ruin all the roots. For this reason the roots should not be put into one large clamp, but two or three smaller ones.

If you have grown those unusual and delicious vegetables, salsify and scorzonera, lift them now. If you prefer, you can leave them in the ground until they are needed. Make sure, however, that they don't get frozen into the ground!

If you have an exposed garden, heel over the earliest broccoli to the north or north-west. This prevents the early morning sun from causing damage when it melts the frost on the centre of the curds.

Greenhouse Have a look at the cinerarias in pots in a deep frame. If they are starting to flower, bring them into the greenhouse; if they are for Christmas, keep them as cool as possible. Pot up any rooted layers of carnations there may be. Pot up also the seedling streptocarpus. Look over the ferns, and if there are any signs of pests dip them in a bucket of water containing derris and a detergent.

The canterbury bells that are going to bloom under glass can be potted up into 15-cm (6-in) pots, and so can the aquilegias (columbines). The cyclamen seedlings should be ready for pricking off into No-Soil potting compost. The annuals should be carefully top-dressed, if they seem to need it, with No-Soil compost. Tie in the shoots of the coleus plants to their canes.

Third weekend

Lawns   This is a good weekend for putting fine sedge peat, often sold as peat-humus, over the lawn; the idea is to provide humus for plants which have had to give up their leaves in the form of grass mowings all through the summer. Having applied the peat evenly, use a broom to distribute it thoroughly.

Go over your lawns with a fork, plunging it into the ground perpendicularly every 60 cm (2 ft) or so, to aerate the ground. This is especially necessary where Mowrah meal has been used to kill worms. Although these creatures are very necessary for the well-being of the garden as a whole, for they enrich the soil, their casts are definitely a nuisance on a lawn. Be sure not to roll the lawn when the ground is wet, or it will become too hard. New lawns can also be laid either this weekend or next.

Flowers   The roots of the blue salvia (salvia patens) and the tall red lobelia (lobelia cardinalis) can be lifted and stored in a frame or cool greenhouse. Put plenty of dry soil or sand in among them. A shady place, say at the base of a north wall, can be used for planting lily of the valley. Put the plants in about 15 cm (6 in) apart in a bed where plenty of sedge peat has been forked in first.

Make certain that slugs do not ruin the pyrethrums, scabious, lupins and delphiniums. With scabious you can put a handful of hydrated lime over the plants, while half a handful is sufficient for the pyrethrum. With delphiniums and lupins, however, coal ashes can be put around the plants.

Fruit   By next week, start planting in earnest. It does not matter

Snails and slugs can be baited with Draza pellets, and the use of powdery compost or sedge peat an inch deep around the plants prevents the slugs from moving in to attack plants

whether it is plums, apples or pears, or any of the soft fruits. They always do much better when they are in the ground at this time of year.

The apples that should be ready for picking this weekend include Bramley's Seedling, Newton Wonder, Reinette du Canada, King of Tomkins County, Annie Elizabeth, Court Pendu Plat, D'Arcy Spice, Duke of Devonshire, Laxton's Pearmain, Lord Lambourne, Dean's Reinette, Ribston Pippin, Wagener and Wellington.

Cuttings can now be taken from redcurrants, which should be treated the same as gooseberries. Take cuttings also of blackcurrants, but do not remove the buds in this case; blackcurrant wood should be inserted 22 cm (9 in) deep, so that only the tips of the shoots are above soil level.

Vegetables Get ready the three-year-old rhubarb crowns for forcing. Lift them now and leave them on the surface of the ground to be touched by the frost. Bring them into the greenhouse and put them underneath the staging, in both dark and heat.

The celery and leeks need their last earthing up either this weekend or next. Kohlrabi can be lifted this week, for they should now be about the size of tennis balls. If they are left in the ground any longer, they tend to get coarse.

Protect globe artichokes by putting coal or coke round each plant, which stops moisture collecting around them. The tops of Jerusalem artichokes can be cut down to within 30 cm (1 ft) of soil level to prevent them blowing over. Dig up the tubers later when there is more time.

Those with a warm south border may like to sow winter spinach. Gardeners in the north can also make a sowing, provided they cover the ground with cloches or frames first and then cover them once the seed is in.

The decaying foliage of seakale should be removed and put on the compost heap, to enable the crowns to ripen. Lift a root of mint this weekend, and put it in a box in the greenhouse or in a heated frame.

Greenhouse Tuberous-rooted begonias should be shaken out, and the tubers arranged upside down on shallow trays for drying off. When they have ripened, the tubers can be stored in any frostproof dry room.

The borders of the greenhouse will be colourful in the winter if they are planted now with myosotis oblongata Blue Bird. In order to put them in, the tomatoes have to be removed. The later varieties of chrysanthemums will need to be disbudded. Continue with this work week by week. Sow some seeds of celosia for summer flowering.

Pot roses should now be pruned and stood out in a frame. The deutzias and philadelphuses can also go into the frames, provided there is sufficient room. Chionodoxa and the tropaeolum tricolour should be potted up this weekend.

Fourth weekend

Two good fruits to eat this weekend would be the pear Marie Louise and the plum President, while Hailshamberry raspberries are usually ready now.

Falling leaves inevitably mean there is a lot of tidying up to do. Put the leaves on the compost heap, sprinkled with a little fish manure, to rot down. If the leaves are left on the beds they may encourage diseases. Remove them also from the lawn and then apply a little dressing of fish manure at the rate of 50 g to the square metre (2 oz to the square yard). Some people now water with a strong hormone to kill the weeds – but it is rather late for this.

Flowers Plant out your spring-flowering forget-me-nots before the tulips, if they are to flower together. Take cuttings of verbena, ageratum and pentstemons in sandy soil in frames. The dahlias will not last much longer than the end of the month, so lift and clean them and store in dry ashes in a frostproof place. Tie in any necessary shoots on wall shrubs.

Any structural alterations in the flower garden can be started now. For instance, erect pergola poles and trellises, make arches, lay paths, build garden steps and so on.

Send in your order for roses. It is far better to plant during the next week or two rather than early in the new year. Prepare a site for a shrub border by digging it over shallowly before the frosts come and make the work impossible.

Fruit Carry out grease-banding of apple, pear and plum trees. Think about clothing any bare patches on the walls or fences by planting more fruit trees and bushes. Order them right away, and plant as soon as possible. Any newly planted trees should be staked so that they do not rock, otherwise they may be killed by the 'wind rocking death' in the winter.

Check over the fruit trees this weekend to see if there are any apples, pears or plums clinging to the branches that are infected by the brown rot disease. If there are, pick them off and drop them into a can of paraffin so that they can be burned easily. If they are not removed, they will become a source of infection next year. As soon as all growth has ceased and the leaves have fallen, start winter pruning.

Vegetables To improve Brussels sprouts, give them a feed of old soot at 125–150 g to the square metre (5–6 oz to the square yard). Make use of an empty frame by planting some parsley in it. Lift the plants with a good ball of soil attached to the roots. They will not flag if transplanted like this. The endives should be blanched; to do this, you can just take a few into a dark shed. A better method is to invert a large pot over a plant, blocking up the drainage hole with either a cork or a lump of clay, so that no light can get in. Another method is to whitewash some cloches and put these over the endive plants.

It is possible to sow a hardy variety of broad bean this weekend. These early sowings are usually free from attacks by black fly or aphis. Cut down the asparagus plants before the berries drop and little seedlings appear all over the ground. It is a good idea to leave one or two plants standing, so that the asparagus beetles congregate on them. After two or three days, dust them with derris and get rid of these pests. The tops of the plants which are cut down can go on the compost heap.

Greenhouse Put on some heat in the greenhouse. Heat is most necessary at night, in order to keep out the frosts. Continue to ventilate in the daytime, provided the weather is all right. As soon as the sun goes down, however, close down the ventilators to conserve any sun heat there may be.

The perpetual-flowering carnations should be disbudded week by week as necessary. Schizanthuses and clarkias should be stopped when they are 10 cm (4 in) high by pinching out the growing points, but mignonettes should be stopped when they are only 5 cm (2 in) high. Few plants are now in active growth and so they will need little water.

November

November brings fog which can do a great deal of harm to plants. See that the greenhouse is properly sealed, block up any cracks with strips of Sylglas tape, and do not open the ventilators during a foggy day. Don't water the plants, because the atmosphere may be very damp. After a severe fog, wash down the glass of the greenhouse thoroughly with hot water containing some liquid detergent.

If you live in an industrial town, or near heavy traffic, you may find you need to syringe the leaves of evergreen plants outside. The idea is to wash off any particles of soot and grime which may block up the breathing pores of the foliage. If any fog should get into a greenhouse, stand in the middle of the floor a large saucerful of ammonia, which acts as an antidote to the plant fumes. If your greenhouse is large, two or three saucers of ammonia may be necessary.

First weekend

General Though mulchings of sedge peat are ideal for all shrubs and should be put on to the depth of 2.5 cm (1 in) all over the ground, you can achieve good results with a 2.5-cm (1-in)-thick layer of freshly fallen leaves. Azaleas, rhododendrons, andromedas and ericaceous plants love such a mulch, and it would be useful to make the application this weekend. Leaves, on the other hand, must be removed from paths, from lawns and from rock gardens – from paths because they make them slippery, from the lawn because the worms will start to pull them in, and from the rock garden because they will smother the choicer alpine plants.

Flowers Start by cleaning up the rock garden. Protect the hairy foliage plants by fixing a little square of glass 7.5 or 10 cm (3 or 4 in) above them to act as a kind of transparent umbrella. Special wires can be bought, or you can hold the glass in position with notched sticks. When you put leaves on to the shrub border, pat them down well with

87

a fork to discourage them from blowing about. Damped sedge peat is more convenient because it never blows about.

Fruit Hopefully, you will have dealt with all the grease-banding of apple, pear and plum trees during the last weekend of October, but if not it should be carried out this weekend. All the apples should have been picked, too, with the exception of May Queen and Underleaf, both of which can be picked this weekend.

Order this weekend the white oil wash you need for spraying in January. Overhaul your spraying machine, if you have one, to make certain that it works perfectly. Trees need to be soaked thoroughly, so don't underestimate the quantity of tar oil you need.

If you are still adopting clean cultivation methods among fruit trees and bushes, fork the soil lightly this weekend to leave it rough. It is much more labour-saving, however, to adopt the straw-mulching method, especially among raspberries and blackcurrants. The first dressing has to be baled straw to the depth of 30 cm (1 ft). Subsequent dressings each year need not usually be more than 7.5 or 10 cm (3 or 4 in). Baled straw is best because it has been bruised during the baling, and so rots down better in the long run. Fish manure is applied over the top of this straw at 75 g to the square metre (3 oz to the square yard).

Vegetables Lift chicory roots for forcing; cut down the leaves to within 2.5 cm (1 in) of the top of the crowns, and then pack them tightly together, crown upwards, in boxes or pots, surrounding them with a mixture of soil and sedge peat in equal parts. Put these prepared roots in a dark, warm place for forcing. It is convenient to do this under the staging of the greenhouse, with a curtain of sacking hung round to keep them dark.

Continue shallow autumn digging this weekend, with the aim of leaving the land rough so that cold winds and frost can act on it. Where you intend growing cabbages, peas and beans, incorporate some really well-rotted compost at one bucketful to the square yard. Bury this about 15 cm (6 in) deep. Don't manure the area to be used for root crops next season – the area for potatoes is best manured at planting time.

Greenhouse Continue disbudding chrysanthemums and give the plants a feed of liquid manure. Repeat the dose the following weekend. Tie in plants as necessary. Watch out for three main troubles: (1) mildew, (2) leaf miner, and (3) aphids. For mildew use Karathane, for leaf miner and aphids use malathion. Sponge any large-leaved foilage plants with a solution of malathion plus liquid detergent.

Do everything possible to encourage reflected light. Paint the hot water pipes white with gloss paint, and whitewash the walls and the edges of the main concrete path.

Lawns   Go over grass verges and make any necessary repairs.

Flowers   Hoe over the soil in the rose garden with the idea of drawing the soil to the bushes rather than away from them. If, however, you are growing roses on the sedge peat mulch system, then just sprinkle on a little extra peat and do not hoe. If there has been any sign of black spot in the summer, gather up the leaves, put them on the compost heap and sprinkle them with a fish fertilizer. The heat produced will kill the spores.

It is still possible to plant galtonia candicans bulbs. It is worthwhile covering the spot where you planted them with some sedge peat, to prevent the frost from doing any damage.

Lightly fork over michaelmas daisy borders after the tops have been cut down. Dahlias should be dug up so that the tubers can be stored. The bed recently vacated can be used for a late planting of wallflowers.

Shrubs and hedges   A lavender hedge makes a pleasing feature in any garden and you can plant one this weekend. There are both tall and short varieties from which to choose.

Go over the shrubs this weekend, and cut out any diseased and dead wood. Don't leave any dead snags to let disease in – snags are the odd ends of wood which can never grow again, and so become a nuisance to the plant. Always cut back, therefore, to the point from which a branch grows or right back to another branch lower down. Make the cut flush with the wood of that branch.

This is a good time to prune a briar hedge. Any new shoots that are needed to thicken it up can be tied in rather than cut off.

Fruit   If you believe in winter pruning, start the moment the leaves are falling. Old fashioned ideas on spur pruning have largely disappeared, with the result that few people today cut back the laterals to within two or three buds of their base and tip the leaders. Today just thin out a branch here and there to let in the light and air. Make certain that there are no rubbing branches and no crossing branches.

Vegetables   Rhubarb and seakale may now be lifted for forcing. With rhubarb it is as well to force only the three- or four-year-old crowns, and to leave them on the top of the soil for two or three weeks so that they are touched by the first frost before being brought into the heat. With seakale pot up three or four good roots in a 17- or 20-cm (7- or 8-in) pot, cover with another pot of a similar size, and bring them into the greenhouse under the staging where there is plenty of heat. Hang some sacking from the staging to make a curtain to keep out the light. Clear the runner beans this weekend, but be sure to leave the roots in the ground, so that the nitrogen they have accumulated in the nodules on their roots can be left where it is needed. It is a simple matter to cut off the stems with a pair of shears at soil level.

There may still be some late beet to harvest and this must be done carefully, as usual, so as not to injure the roots and make them bleed. Once the tops have been twisted off carefully, the roots can be stored in a clamp.

Greenhouse   Continue to take cuttings of perpetual-flowering carnations, to produce plants that will flower in the winter. Examine the bulbs that are now in their standing ground covered with sand or sedge peat. Roman hyacinths and prepared hyacinths should now be ready to come into the greenhouse, as well as the early-flowering tulips. Some of the polyanthus types of narcissi will be ready to bring in for forcing. If you have bought specially retarded lily of the valley crowns, these can be brought into the heated greenhouse now for forcing.

Primula obconicas will probably want potting on into 15-cm (6-in) pots, and the flowering stocks should go into 15-cm (6-in) pots this weekend, too. Cinerarias will need to be housed in the greenhouse, and hippeastrums should go into the greenhouse also at a temperature of 13°C (55°F). Any that need re-potting should be attended to. At the same time the lilium henrii should be potted up, while coleus that are large enough should be potted on from 7.5-cm (3-in) to 15-cm (6-in) pots.

Third weekend

General Don't wait until December before thinking about Christmas presents. Maybe you wants to give some pot plants, and if so they will need growing on carefully.

If the weekend is wet, sharpen the blades of the hoes, spades and mattocks with a file.

Lawns Give the lawns a light raking with a spring-tined rake, often sold as a Springbok. Remove any moss and weeds to the compost heap. Then apply a mercury dressing to kill the moss for good. Follow this with a good brushing with a broom to stimulate the grass.

While thinking of the lawn, overhaul your mower. The blades will certainly need sharpening.

Flowers It is convenient to plant ranunculus and anemone coronaria this weekend. As I have already said in connection with other bulbs, it does give protection if a dressing of sedge peat or bracken is put on the soil afterwards – protection not only against frost but also to prevent the rain from beating the soil down hard.

Shrubs and hedges Don't forget that if evergreens were planted recently, that they will need some shelter. Put a screen of sacking round them.

Fruit Fruit trees that have been making nothing but wood and not producing fruit at all, and are over, say, ten years old, may be root pruned. The idea is to dig a trench around one side of the tree about 90 cm (3 ft) away and about 60–90 cm (2–3 ft) deep. During the operation cut out neatly any roots that cross the trench. Treat the other side of the tree in the same way the following year. Fig trees often succeed best when they are root pruned every November. In northern districts it may be necessary to protect the branches of the trees by hanging mats over them.

This weekend, start planting fruit trees and bushes. Put in the gooseberries first and then plant the other fruits in the following order: (1) morello cherries, (2) sweet cherries, (3) plums, (4) pears, (5) apples, (6) raspberries, (7) blackcurrants, and (8) redcurrants. It is important to plant firmly and, generally speaking, shallowly. Shallow planting is especially important in the case of grafted apples, pears and plums. If grafted trees are planted too deeply, then what is called 'scion rooting' takes place. This completely masks all the effects which the roots of the stocks should have made.

Do not dig in old manure or compost before planting except in the case of soft fruits. With hard fruits, it is better to apply compost or straw afterwards as a mulch. It is difficult to plant firmly in land that has been enriched with quantities of compost.

Vegetables Continue to blanch endive plants that are full size; cover individual plants with large upturned pots or cardboard boxes instead. A fully-formed endive takes three weeks to blanch this way. To get continuity, cover a few plants each weekend. When the seakale is lifted the side roots should be cut off – they make the thongs which are planted out next spring. Keep these 10-cm (4-in) thongs in bundles in the open, covered with sand.

Lightly hoe over the soil in frames where lettuces are growing, and where cauliflower plants are over-wintering. Use a bent two-pronged fork, and just scratch the soil lightly. This prevents moss from forming and lets in a little air.

Greenhouse If you are growing large incurved Japanese chrysanthemums, be prepared to take cuttings this weekend or next. They root quickly at this time. Sow the seeds of alpine plants in pots filled with a sandy peaty compost. Leave them outside plunged in the soil so that they can be covered with snow for a fortnight or more before they go into the cold frame. Prune the vines under glass this weekend; butting the laterals to within one eye of their base, and then wash the rods down with a 5 per cent tar oil wash. If you have been raising asparagus plumosus from seed, pot up the little plants into their 7.5-cm (3-in) pots, using No-Soil potting compost.

The earliest-flowering azaleas should now go into the greenhouse at a temperature of 13°C (55°F). Give the cyclamen a feed of diluted liquid manure. Pot on the herbaceous calceolarias into 15-cm (6-in) pots with No-Soil potting compost. Don't coddle the plants at this time of the year; be prepared to ventilate whenever the weather makes it possible. Introduce the clivias into the greenhouse at a temperature of 13°C (55°F). Put a top dressing of No-Soil potting compost over the soil in each case.

Fourth weekend

General This is a very good weekend for making up mushroom beds. Compost can be bought ready for planting up, and mushrooms can be grown quite successfully in boxes in the kitchen.

Collect all the leaves you can this weekend for making into good compost with an activator like fish manure. If bracken grows near you, go and cut some and put it on the compost heap.

Flowers Any hardy climbers needed to cover fences or walls should be planted now. Also supply your garden pool with the plants you need. Christmas roses must be protected from cold and wet; a square cloche or glass frame put over the top is the ideal protection, for it keeps off excessive rain and yet gives automatic ventilation.

Those who forgot to take briar cuttings in October may like to know that there is still time to do so this weekend. Herbaceous borders can be planted but the soil should be forked first, and well-rotted compost should be added at a bucketful to the square yard.

Shrubs and hedges Magnolias can do with a top-dressing of leaves or sedge peat this weekend. Put them round the stems of the bushes, in a ring about 1.25 metres (4 ft) wide.

Fruit If you have an old neglected orchard, start pruning it this weekend. The main idea is to saw out the rubbing and crossing branches and the dead and diseased wood. Branches in the centre of the tree that keep out the light and air should be carefully removed. If any big saw cuts are made, clean them up afterwards with a sharp knife, to leave them smooth. Then paint them over with Stockholm tar.

Morello cherries do best on north walls. Plant the fan-trained specimens now or, if they are already established, prune them. Cut out the old wood and tie in all the young whippy new wood. These little one-year-old branches should be spaced out about 10 cm (4 in) apart. Get this work done as soon as possible, and then the trees will be ready for spraying with a tar oil wash early in December.

Vegetables Lime should be applied as a top dressing to land that has been dug. To know the exact amount to apply, test the soil with a BDH soil indicator, and then give the quantity indicated. Most gardeners find carbonate of lime convenient to use.

It should be possible to lift parsnips now, and the strip of ground can then be dug. Parsnip roots may always be left on the surface of the ground in a heap, for they are not ruined by frost – they are often improved by it.

It is possible to sow a hardy variety of pea, such as Meteor, out of doors this weekend. Treat the seed before sowing with an organo-mercury dust. This is a far better proposition in the warmer parts of the south than in the north, though even in the north the peas will survive under continuous cloches. If the rows of autumn-sown onions have got weedy, you may have to hand weed – and this can only be done if the ground is not too sodden. Try and get the onion rows cleaned up, however, before the winter sets in. Horseradish thongs can be planted in raised beds this weekend.

Greenhouse The rhubarb roots that were dug up some time ago and have been sitting on the ground can now be put under the staging of the greenhouse, as close together as possible, with some damp sedge peat packed in between. They must be kept in the dark, have some heat, and from time to time be syringed over to keep them moist. Keep forcing the seakale roots.

The late peach trees growing in the greenhouse should now be pruned. The aim here is to cut out much of the old wood, and to retain the shorter lengths of young wood which will fruit. If you want to start peach trees, now is the time to plant fan-trained specimens in the borders prepared for the purpose.

If you grow lettuces in the borders of your greenhouses – varieties like Cheshunt Early Giant – water carefully in between the plants through a fine rose. If the leaves are kept turgid, they will be held just off the soil, and this will prevent them from having a bad attack of botrytis disease.

Some people like an early crop of tomatoes, and this weekend they should sow, in No-Soil seed compost, the seeds of a variety like Grower's Pride. The moment the young seedlings come through in, say, a fortnight's time, they should be potted up into 7.5-cm (3-in) pots with No-Soil potting compost or, better still, they should be set in soil blocks. The pots or soil blocks should then be put on a shelf near the glass roof of the greenhouse at a temperature of about 15°C (60°F). This will prevent them from growing long and leggy.

December

First weekend

General   If November has been kind, you can usually rely on severe frosts in December. Pay particular attention to outside taps, pipes and pumps. Frames may need to have protection during frosty weather, especially if there is no means of heating them, and if they are growing half-hardly plants.

Scrape your boots free of soil when stepping off the garden on to gravel paths – soil does them no good at all.

If you have a pool in the garden, plant specimens which like damp conditions all around the edge. It should be possible to attend to paths. A gravel path may need rolling to firm it and so may an ash path, while there may even be some weeds to be eliminated.

Flowers   You can now plant almost all kinds of roses. Think seriously about the floribunda types, which go on flowering from June until early October and which make a wonderful show with the minimum of work. Remember that you get the best results by covering the ground with sedge peat to the depth of 2.5 cm (1 in). This not only creates the perfect mulch, but provides the organic matter that roses need, and saves having to hoe during the summer.

It very much depends upon the weather what can be done this weekend. If it remains fine then some of the hardy herbaceous specimens can be planted to make a beautiful border.

Fruit   If the weekend is fine, start the tar distillate spraying. Even if the pruning has not been completed, get the spraying done. Buy a tar oil wash such as Mortegg which will destroy the eggs of a number of fruit tree pests like the aphids suckers; in addition it will drastically reduce attacks by spring caterpillars. A tar oil wash, however, not only kills insect eggs but it also gets rid of woolly aphis, and kills the moss and lichen on trunks and branches. The trees and bushes must be given a thorough soaking. Trees that have not been sprayed for years need to be sprayed with a 10 per cent solution but, where winter spraying has been carried out each December, a 5 per cent solution should do. Spray all types of fruit trees and bushes with such a wash, but no nut bushes or strawberry plants.

Concentrate on the pruning, if it has not already been completed. It is always better to do the winter tar oil washing in December, and if the pruning is done first there is less wood to cover. Burn all the prunings, and sprinkle the cold ashes along the rows of gooseberries, redcurrants and raspberries. Take an interest in the pruning – don't make mistakes. The redcurrant bush, for instance, bears on short spurs of the old wood, while the blackcurrant produces its fruit on the new.

Vegetables Use any spare time this weekend to clear away all the crops as they cease to be of value. Pull up the stumps of winter cabbages and cauliflowers, for instance, and bash them up with the back of an axe before putting them on the compost heap. Don't leave them in the ground, because they rob it of plant food.

Greenhouse If you didn't sow tomato seeds earlier on, do so this weekend. The aim is to produce plants for setting out in the heated greenhouse about the middle of March.

Those who managed to sow their sweet peas in November should now find the plants ready for potting on into 7.5-cm (3-in) pots, using No-Soil potting compost. Some people, however, prefer to put the little plants into soil blocks.

By the end of the month it should be possible to start forcing hydrangeas in pots. These should be given a good watering and a good syringing over, and they can be stood on the staging of the greenhouse at a temperature of 15°C (60°F). Those who like very early French beans should sow some seeds of the variety Processor in a 15-cm (6-in) pot. Six seeds should be sown 2.5 cm (1 in) deep around the edge of the pot; the seedlings are thinned down to four or five later. The beans will be grown on in the greenhouse at a temperature of 13–15°C (55–60°F).

Second weekend
General Reset any edging stones that have come out of place. If any

particular part of the garden appears to be badly drained, during this weekend and the next trenches can be dug and agricultural drainpipes laid down.

Flowers   The iris stylosa may be coming into flower, and slugs are particularly partial to the stems as they appear. Protection should therefore be given with blue Draza pellets.

Shrubs and hedges   In some gardens there are too many old, rather dull evergreen shrubs, and this is a good weekend to eliminate them. The branches can be used for house decoration at Christmas. Plant beautiful flowering shrubs in their place.

Any snow should be knocked off the branches of shrubs and trees, or the weight of it may break the branches.

Fruit   See that all the young trees are properly staked. Too often the tree supports the stake, and not the stake the tree. Make certain that none of the ties are strangling the trunks.

Unfortunately some of the pests and diseases that attack our fruit trees and bushes come from the hedgerows. This is especially true with such hedging plants as myrobalan, sloe or quick. It is therefore worthwhile spraying the hedge thoroughly with a 5 per cent tar oil wash, as well as spraying the fruit trees and bushes. Apply the wash with pressure and force. First clear up the debris underneath the hedge, where pests may lurk.

Vegetables   When the rows of runner beans, French beans, broad beans and peas are cleared, remember to cut the stems off at soil level, to leave the roots in the ground. These roots have nitrogenous nodules on them which benefit the soil immediately. Pull up the peasticks and beanpoles, and stand them upside down in bundles to dry off. When buying new peasticks and beanpoles, dip the bases in Rentokil green wood preservative and they will last far longer. The green wood preservative can be put into a large container, and the poles or sticks stood in the liquid for a day or two.

Ventilate the cauliflowers that are growing in cold frames, and remove any decaying leaves. Dust the plants with a fine Karathane dust, such as that used for cinerarias.

Greenhouse   If the cinerarias are growing well, they will need more room for development, so space the pots out now to give at least 2.5 cm (1 in) of room between the leaves of one plant and the next. If necessary, dust with one of the fine Karathane dusts to prevent mildew. Cut the late chrysanthemums for house decoration. Decide which stools to keep for propagation purposes. Each stool should give six cuttings. Stools that are not required can be thrown on to the compost heap. Curiously enough, the later the variety of chrysanthemum, the earlier the cuttings have to be taken. Start this weekend with the really late kinds, and strike the cuttings in a box filled with a mixture of coarse silver sand and sedge peat. Put glass and a sheet of paper over the box, and stand it on the staging of the greenhouse at a temperature of 15°C (60°F).

If you are growing godetias in 5-cm (2-in) pots, these should now be potted on into 15-cm (6-in) pots. The earlier-struck pelargoniums may also be ready for potting on into 15-cm (6-in) pots. Don't forget that it is always possible to take cuttings of these plants over an extended period, so that they become ready for potting on at different times. With this in mind, take some cuttings this weekend.

If there is room, take some of the flowering chrysanthemum plants into the house now.

Third weekend
General   If the weather is kind, lay down paving stones or make a crazy-paving or brick path. Gravel paths are best made at this time of the year also, and they invariably set well in a damp period, after a good rolling.

Do any necessary repairs to tools. The handles should be oiled with linseed oil, and the blades with a mineral oil. Sharpen hoes, sickles and scythes. Give the garden shed a good clean out. Repair all the seed boxes, and then dip them in a solution of Rentokil green wood preservative which will make them last longer. False bottoms to these boxes may be made with strips of plastic material if necessary.

Lawns   It is possible to lay down turves to form a grass path, or even a complete lawn. Don't attempt to do this, however, unless the soil is nice and friable. Prick the soil over to the depth of 5 or 7.5 cm (2 or 3 in), see that it is absolutely level, lay the turves neatly in position, and beat them down with a wooden beater.

Shrubs and hedges   If you are cutting holly and other evergreens for Christmas decoration, take care that the branches are not injured, and that the shape of the bushes is not spoiled.

This is really not a good weekend to prune evergreens, and so the less done at this time of the year the better. Continue to make sure that shrubs are firmly staked (see below).

Fruit   Check over the apples and pears in store and, if there are any diseased ones, throw them out. Remember that it is possible for the storehouse to be too dry, in which case the apples and pears will shrivel. If this happens, sprinkle the floor with water to create a more humid atmosphere, and the fruit should plump up again.

Continue to attend to the staking of your fruit trees and flowering trees. If they are allowed to rock even slightly during the winter, a little cone-shaped depression will be formed at the base of the main stem which will fill up with water. This will kill the tops of the roots at this point, and because they cannot breathe, the tree will die.

Vegetables   Succession with forced seakale, chicory and rhubarb is obtained by bringing in the plants at regular intervals. Try lifting and forcing this weekend, and cover up some more endive for blanching. Look over the root crops in store and see if any are going bad – remove them immediately before they contaminate the rest of the heap. If beetroot is shrivelling the problem is over-dryness, as mentioned earlier in the case of apples and pears. Syringe the roots with a little water.

If the ground is hard and frozen this weekend, you have an excellent opportunity for wheeling out barrow-loads of compost and placing heaps in positions where it will be needed for digging in later on. Remove decaying leaves of Brussels sprouts and other winter greens before disease takes charge. Once they are yellow they are of no value to the plant, and they are better on the compost heap. Protect the celery this weekend by covering the tops with cloches or by using some dried bracken. The idea is to prevent the rain from seeping down into the hearts of the plants, where it may rot them.

Greenhouse   The moment the schizanthus plants are starting to branch, provide a few peasticks to keep them upright. If you failed to stop them in November, do so this weekend.

Take the bulbs from underneath their ashes or sand in the open, or out of a dark cupboard, and bring them into the greenhouse or home for growing on in the light. As a general rule bulbs need to be in the dark for ten or eleven weeks before any attempt is made to force them. Next weekend there will probably be some more daffodils to bring in, as well as some more hyacinths. By bringing them in in succession like this you can be certain that they will flower in succession, too. Chionodoxas can be brought into the greenhouse this weekend also.

Attend to the cactus and succulents, i.e. remove with a pointed stick any moss growing around the plants. These plants will need very little watering at this time of year, so put them on a shelf where they can get plenty of light and give them a drop of water once a month or so.

Fourth weekend

General Round about Christmas-time few people do much gardening. In the greenhouse, be very careful about watering – water can be splashed about in the summer, but never in the winter. Give a little ventilation, unless it is very foggy when it is a good thing to close the vents completely. Never make the mistake, however, of trying to save fuel by keeping the greenhouse closed up. This encourages disease. The most important thing of all is to have the glass clean, so that the plants can get all the light they need. Then the plants must have a change of air from time to time. It helps also if the pots are clean, so always soak new pots in clean water before using them, to save watering later. Give old pots a good scrubbing and washing before using them again.

Flowers What about a heather garden? This is the simplest and cheapest form of flower gardening there is, from the labour point of view. There are heathers which suit acid soils, and others which are equally happy in soils containing lime.

A little armchair gardening does no harm this weekend. Read about making better herbaceous borders, or how to create a magnificent flowering shrub border, etc. Plans can be made for replanting, and it is a good thing to think seriously about systems of bedding out. Browse through seed catalogues and start to make out your orders.

Fruit In the case of top fruits, sow the soil with grass which will only have to be mown regularly instead of having to be constantly hoed. Furthermore, better-flavoured and more highly-coloured dessert apples are assured on grassland than on cultivated soil. With soft fruits, consider using straw 30 cm (1 ft) deep. The alternative to baled straw would be sedge peat.

Vegetables Armchair gardening and planning again.

Greenhouse There is little to do this weekend, other than the routine work described in the general section above. There may be decaying leaves to remove, and you will probably need to cut some flowers that are past their best. Keep an eye on ventilation. Watering will be reduced to a bare minimum. If you grow vines and peaches in the greenhouse you should continue pruning and spraying. The rhubarb and seakale under the staging of the house should be syringed over with tepid water, while the pot covering the chicons of chicory should be removed for an hour or two to warm the soil holding the roots upright.

Charts and tables

Unusual fruits and vegetables

Apple cucumbers Can be grown up tall bamboos or poles. Fruits large as goose eggs.

Asparagus peas Grow like dwarf peas. Pick the pods when young, and cook whole.

Aubergines Also called egg plants. Grow as tomatoes, and cook the large purple fruits by baking or cut up and fried.

Blue-podded beans Turn a rich green colour after 2 minutes in boiling water.

Boysenberries Larger fruit than the loganberry. Very delicious; ripe in August.

Capsicum Large red or green fruits. Used cut up raw in salads, and cooked in curries.

Cardoon Grow like celery in trenches, and are blanched. Cook in steam or boiling water.

Celtuce Leaves used like lettuce and the heart like celery.

Chinese cabbage Like a cos lettuce. Use raw in salads, or cook in boiling water.

Colewort A very small cabbage. Ready in November.

Courgettes Like very small marrows. Cook whole, or cut up and fry or grill.

Couve tronchuda Cabbage with thick white centres to its leaves.

Good King Henry Use the young shoots as asparagus to start with, and then the leaves as spinach.

Kohlrabi Root vegetable like a turnip but more delicious. Use in autumn or winter.

Lima beans Thresh out the beans and boil for only a few minutes. Taste is similar to roasted chestnuts.

Nectarberries A type of loganberry. Ripe in August.

New Zealand spinach Plant that creeps along the top of the soil like ground ivy.

Okra Cook the young green and yellow seed vessels. Useful for soups and stews.

Salsify Longish white roots. Clean and boil, and eat with white sauce.

Scoronera Longish black roots. Use in winter. Treat as salsify.

Seakale spinach Thick white stems cooked like seakale. Dark green leaves cooked like spinach.

Skirret Use the roots as carrots in autumn and winter.

Soya beans Fiskebury V is the best variety. Sow early June 7·5 cm (3 in) apart. Cook as haricot beans.

Squashes Large fruits like marrow, and the same method should be used for cooking.

Sugar peas Also known as mange tout. Pick the pods when young and cook whole.

Tic beans Eat as green beans when young, or thresh out dry beans in the autumn and boil them.

Worcesterberries Grows like a gooseberry, but has small red fruits like redcurrants.

Diseases and pests

Aphids Includes greenfly, blue fly and mealy blue fly. Attacks all kinds of plants. Spray or dust with derris.

Big bud Tiny mite which attacks the buds of blackcurrants, causing them to swell. Spray with lime-sulphur when the leaves are about 2·5 cm (1 in) across.

Black leg Occurs in beetroot and geraniums. In the former, treat the seed with an organic mercury compound, and, in the latter, water with a dilution of Chestnut compound.

Black spot A disease of roses, where the leaves develop black spots. Spray with a Captan wash called 'Fuclasin'.

Brown rot A disease which attacks apples, causing them to rot. Pick off all the affected specimens and compost them properly. Spray the trees as for scab.

Cabbage root fly· Attacks the roots of cabbages, cauliflowers, etc. Lay down small squares of tarred felt to catch them.

Club root A disease which ruins the roots of cabbages, cauliflowers,

Brussels sprouts, etc. Put a small piece of garlic into each hole at planting time.

Codling moth A maggot which tunnels into apples. Apply pieces of corrugated paper, ridged-side down, around the trunks of the trees in July; these will trap the maggots as they descend to pupate. Take off and burn the cardboard in October.

Flea beetle A tiny beetle which nibbles the leaves of cabbage seedlings, turnips, swedes, etc. Dust liberally with derris.

Leaf miners Little maggots which tunnel into leaves of chrysanthemums and cinerarias. Spray with Malathion.

Mildew A powdery white substance which attacks leaves and stems. Spray with karathane.

Onion fly Its maggots ruin the bulbs of onions. Sow carrots and onions in alternate rows – the smell of the carrots will keep onion fly away.

Peach leaf curl Plant garlic cloves all around the tree at a distance of 90 cm (3 ft).

Potato blight Kills the leaves of the potato. Spray in July with Bordeaux mixture before the attack comes, then 5 days later, and again if necessary.

Red spider Tiny red mites which suck the undersides of leaves of many plants, especially apples, peaches, vines and chrysanthemums. Spray with derris.

Rust A browny-red powdery substance usually found on the undersides of leaves. Spray with derris.

Scab Brownish-black spots on apples and pears. Spray with lime-sulphur at 1 in 30 just before the blossoms open, and at 1 in 60 when all the petals have fallen.

Winter moth Its caterpillars eat the leaves of apple trees. Spray with pyrethrum.

Woolly aphis A white wool-like substance on apple trees. Paint with neat liquid derris.

Seed longevity

	Years		years
Artichoke, globe	3–4	Basil	8
Asparagus	3	Beans	3
Beet	6	Marjoram, winter	5
Borage	8	Marrows	3

	years		years
Broccoli	5	Melons	5
Brussels sprouts	5	Mustard	4
Cabbage	5	Onion	2
Cardoons	7	Parsley	3
Carrots	4	Parsnip	2
Cauliflower	5	Peas	3
Celery	4	Pumpkins	3
Chard, Swiss	4	Radish	5
Chervil	1	Rhubarb	3
Chicory	8	Rosemary	4
Chives	3	Sage	3
Corn, sweet	3	Salsify	2
Couve tronchuda	3	Savory, summer or winter	3
Cress	5	Savoy	5
Cucumber	6	Scorzonera	2
Endive	10	Seakale	1
Fennel	4	Spinach (all varieties)	5
Kale	4	Swede	5
Kohlrabi	5	Thyme	3
Leeks	3	Tomatoes	4
Lettuce	5	Turnip	5
Marjoram, sweet	3		

Length of seed germination

	days		days
Asparagus	14–21	Lettuce	6–10
Beans	7–14	Marrow, vegetable (outdoor)	7–14
Beet	10–18	Marrow, vegetable (in heat)	3–5
Broccoli	5–10	Melons (in heat)	3–6
Brussels sprouts	5–10	Mustard	3–4
Cabbage	5–10	Onion	10–16
Carrots	12–18	Parsley	15–26
Cauliflower	5–10	Parsnip	10–20
Chicory	5–10	Peas	7–14
Cress	4–6	Radishes	3–6
Cucumbers (outdoor)	7–14	Savoy	5–10
Cucumbers (in heat)	2–4	Spinach	7–10
Endive	5–14	Tomatoes (in heat)	6–10
Leeks	10–14	Turnips	4–10

Planning your vegetable garden (sowing and planting chart)

Crop	Varieties	Sow (s)* Plant (p)*	Cover	Harvest	No. of rows	Distances in row in cm (in)
Aubergines	Early Long Purple	p May	May–Sept	Aug/Sept	1	45 (18)
Beans, broad	Claudia Aquadulce	s Jan	Jan–April	May/June	2	20 (8)
Beans, dwarf	Masterpiece	s Late March	March–May	June	2	15 (6)
		s July	Oct–Nov	Oct/Nov	2	20 (8)
Beans, runner	Streamline	s Late March	March–May	June	2	20 (8)
Beetroot	Any globe variety	s Late March	March–April	May/June	4	10 (4)
Spring cabbage	Harbinger	s Late July	Jan–March	March	2	45 (18)
Carrots	Early Nantes	s Oct	Oct–March	May	5	5 (2)
		s Jan–March	Jan–March	May	5	5 (2)
Cauliflower	All year round	s End Sept	April	June	3	45 (18)
	Snowball	s Jan	April	June	5	45 (18)
Cucumbers	Conqueror	p May	May–Sept	July/Sept	2	60–90 (24–36)
Lettuce, autumn	Arctic King	s Aug	Oct–Dec.	Nov/Dec	4	22 (9)
Lettuce, winter	May King	s Oct	Oct–April	March–April	4	22 (9)
Lettuce, spring	Unrivalled	s Jan–Feb	Jan–April	May	4	22 (9)
	May Queen	p Jan	Jan–April	April	4	22 (9)
Marrow	Green Bush	p April	April–May	June	1	60 (24)
Onions	White Lisbon	s Sept	Oct–March	March	5	5 (2)
Peas	Kelvedon Wonder	s Nov–Jan	Nov–May	May	4	5 (2)
Peppers	Meteor Outdoor	p Late May	May–Sept		1	45 (18)
Radish	French Breakfast	s Dec–March	Dec–April	April	4	1 (½)
		s Sept	Oct.–Dec	Nov/Dec	4	1 (½)
Sweet corn	North Star	s April	April–May	July	1	22 (9)
Tomatoes (bush)	Amateur	p April	April–Sept	Aug–Sept	2	60 (24)

*Those who live north of Manchester may have to sow and plant a month later

Summer flowers

Name	Colour of flowers	Hardy or half-hardy	Height in inches	Place to sow	Sowing time	Planting out time	Distances (planting) in cm(in)	(thinning) in cm(in)
Ageratum	Pink, blue, mauve	HHA	6–12	G	March	May	15–20(6–8)	10–15(4–6)
Alyssum	White, violet	HA	2–6	O	March–May		30(12)	
Amaranthus	Red, green	HHA	24	G	Feb–March	May	15–30(6–12)	
Antirrhinum	Various	HHA	18	G	Jan.–March	May	30 (12)	
Arctotis	Yellow, white, orange	HHA	18	O	Feb–March	May		30(12)
Bartonia	Yellow	HA	18	O	March			
Brachycome	Blue, white	HHA	9	G	March	May	22(9)	
Calendula	Orange, yellow	HA	12–15	O	March–May & Sept		30(12)	
Candytuft	White to purple	HA	12	O	March–May & Sept		30(12)	
Chrysanthemum	Maroon, yellow, white, scarlet	HA	18	O	March–May & Sept		30(12)	
Clarkia	Pink, white, crimson	HA	24	O	March–May		22(9)	
Cobaea scandens	Purple	HHA	Climber	G	Feb–March	May–June	90(36)	
Convolvulus	Crimson, white, purple	HA	Trailer	O	April–May		25(10)	
Cosmea	Pink, crimson, orange, white	HHA	36	G	Feb–March	May–June	30(12)	
Cornflower	Rose, white, blue	HA	24	O	March–April & Sept		22(9)	

G = Greenhouse   O = Outside

Summer flowers (continued)

Name	Colour of flowers	Hardy or half-hardy	Height in inches	Place to sow	Sowing time	Planting out time	Distances (planting) in cm(in)	(thinning) in cm(in)
Dianthus (carnation)	White to crimson	HHA	9–12	G	Feb–March	May–June	22(9)	
Dimorphotheca	Beige, orange, salmon	HHA	12	G	March–April	May	22–30(9–12)	
Errcremocarpus	Scarlet, orange	HHA	Climber	G	Feb–March	May	90(36)	
Eschscholzia	Yellow, carmine	HA	10–12	O	March–May		22(9)	
Godetia	White, crimson, pink	HA	12–24	O	March–May		22(9)	
Gypsophilia	White, carmine	HA	12	O	March–May		22(9)	
Impatiens	Orange, crimson, white	HHA	12	O	Feb–March	May	22–30(9–12)	
Kockia	Ferny foliage turning crimson	HHA	24	G	Feb–March	May	30(12)	
Larkspur	White, blue, pink, scarlet	HA	24	O	April & Sept			37(15)
Lavatera	White and rose	HA	30	O	March–April			45(18)
Leptosiphon	Yellow, orange, pink, red	HA	6	O	April–May			15(6)
Linum	Scarlet	HA	9	O	March–May			15(6)
Lobelia	Blue, carmine	HHA	6	G	March	May	15(6)	
Lupin	Ping, crimson, blue, white	HA	24	O	March–May			30(12)
Marigold (African or French)	Yellow or orange	HHA	12–24	G	April	May	15–30(6–12)	
Mesembryanthemum	Various	HHA	Trailer	G	April	May	22(9)	
Mignonette	Greenish-yellow, red, white	HA	18	O	March–May		22(9)	

Nasturtium	Yellow to crimson	HA	9 or Climber	O	April		22(9)
Nemesia	Various	HHA	12	G	Feb–March	May	15–20(6–8)
Nemophilia	Blue	HA	6	O	April		15(6)
Nicotiana	White, pink, crimson	HHA	24	G	March	May	30(12)
Nigella	White, pink, blue	HA	18	O	April		30(12)
Petunia	White, pink, purple, blue	HHA	6–12	G	March–April	May	20–30(8–12)
Phacelia	Blue	HA	9	O	April–May	May	22(9)
Phlox	Various	HHA	12	G	March	May	22(9)
Poppy	Various	HA	18–25	O	April–May	May	30(12)
Salpiglossis	Various	HHA	24	G	Feb–March	May	30(12)
Saponaria	Rose	HA	6	O	April–May	May	15(6)
Scabious	White, pink, maroon, lavender	HA	20–24	G & O	April–May	June	27(11)
Stocks	Various	HHA	15–18	G	March–April	May	30(12)
Sunflower	Yellow, orange, coppery-red	HA	120	O	March–April	May	60(24)
Sweet Pea	Various	HA	Climber	G & O	April or Sept under glass	April	22 (9)
Sweet Sultan	White, purple, rose	HA	18	O	April	May	22(9)
Tagetes	Yellow, orange	HHA	9	G	April	May	15(6)
Ursinia	Orange	HHA	12	G	April	May	22–30(9–12)
Venidiums	Various	HHA	18	G	April	May	30–45(12–18)
Virginia Stock	Various	HA	6	O	April–May		10(4)
Viscaria	White, crimson, blue, pink	HA	12	O	April–May		15(6)

G = Greenhouse   O = Outside

Greenhouse shrubs and perennials

Name	Colours possible	Season in bloom	Remarks
Abutilon striatum	Orange flowers	Summer	Prune hard in March
Acacia dealbata (mimosa)	Yellow	Spring	Prune fairly hard after flowering
Azalea indica	Pink and crimson	Early winter and spring	Pink outside in the summer
Boronia megastigma	Maroon and yellow	Spring	Fragrant
Callistemon citrinus	Red	Summer	Like bottle brushes
Campanula isophylla	Blue	July–August	A trailing plant
Carnations	Red, pink and yellow	All year round	In 15-cm (6-in) pots
Cassia corymbosa	Yellow	Summer	Prune hard in winter
Citrus mitis (baby orange)	Orange fruits	All year round	Orange fruits
Erythrina crista-gallii	Scarlet	Summer	There is a dwarf kind
Felicia amelloides (marguerite)	Blue	Summer	Raised from cuttings
Francoa ramosa (bridal wreath)	White	July–Aug	Raised from seed
Fuschia	Red, pink and purple	July–Oct	Many varieties
Gerbera jamesonii	Red and orange	Summer	South African flowers
Kalanchoe	Red or yellow	Spring and summer	Small compact types
Lagerstroemia indica	Rose-pink flowers	Mid-summer	Prune in spring
Lantana	Yellow, pink and orange	Summer	Various varieties
Luculia gratissima	Pink	December	Prune in spring
Mimosa pudica	Pink	Summer	Sow seeds in spring
Oleander	Red, pink and white	Summer	Prune each year after flowering

Pelargoniums	Pink, red and bluish	Spring	Various varieties	
Rochea coccinea	Red	July and Aug	Tubular flowers	
Solanum capsicastrum	Orange berries	All winter	Sow seed in spring	
Streptocarpus	Blue, pink and white	July–Sept	Take leaf cuttings	

Flowering shrubs and month of flowering

Latin name	Common name	Colour	Height in m(ft)	Spread in m(ft)	
January					
Chimonanthus praecox	Winter Sweet	Primrose	2·5 (8)	1·5 (5)	D
Erica carnea gracilis	Heather	Rose-pink	·3 (1)	·6 (2)	E
Garrya elliptica	Tassel Bush	Jade-green	2·5 (8)	2·5 (8)	E
Hamamelis mollis	Witch Hazel	Yellow	2·5 (8)	2·5 (8)	D
Lonicera fragrantissima	Honeysuckle	Cream	1·8 (6)	2·1 (7)	SE
Mahonia japonica	Berberis	Primrose	1·8 (6)	2·1 (7)	E
Viburnum fragrans	Viburnum	Pale pink	2·75(9)	2·5 (8)	D
Viburnum tinus	Laurustinus	White	2·5 (8)	2·1 (7)	E
February					
Camellia japonica	Camellia	Various	3 (10)	3(10)	E
Chimonanthus praecox	Winter Sweet	Primrose	2·5 (8)	1·5 (5)	D
Daphne mezereum	Daphne	Purple	·9 (3)	1·2 (4)	E
Erica darleyensis	Heather	Rose-purple	·6 (2)	·6 (2)	E

Flowering shrubs and month of flowering (continued)

Latin name	Common name	Colour	Height in m(ft)	Spread in m(ft)	
Hamamelis mollis	Witch Hazel	Yellow	2·5 (8)	2·5 (8)	D
Lonicera fragrantissima	Honeysuckle	Cream	1·8 (6)	2·1 (7)	SE
Mahonia japonica	Berberis	Primrose	1·8 (6)	2·1 (7)	E
Viburnum bodnantense	Viburnum	Deep rose	3(10)	2·5 (8)	D
March					
Camellia williamsii	Camellia	Pink	2·5 (8)	2·5 (8)	E
Chaenomeles speciosa	Japanese Quince	Pink, red, white	1·8 (6)	2·75(9)	D
Erica arborea alpina	Tree Heath	White	1·8 (6)	·9 (3)	E
Erica mediterranea	Heather	White to purple	·9 (3)	1·5 (5)	E
Forsythia Lynwood	Golden Bells	Yellow	2·1 (7)	2·1 (7)	D
Magnolia stellata	Star Magnolia	White	2·1 (7)	2·1 (7)	D
Mahonia aquifolium	Large-leaved Berberis	Yellow	·9 (3)	1·5 (5)	E
Pieris floribunda	Lily of the Valley Shrub	White	1·5 (5)	1·8 (6)	E
Rhododendron praecox	Rhododendron	Rose-mauve	·9 (3)	1·5 (5)	E
Spiraea thunbergii	Bridal Wreath	White	1·5 (5)	1·5 (5)	E
Ulex europaeus plenus	Double Gorse	Yellow	2·5 (8)	1·8 (6)	E
April					
Azalea amoenum	Japanese Azalea	Carmine	·9 (3)	1·2 (4)	D
Berberis darwinii	Barberry	Orange	2·1 (7)	2·1 (7)	E
Berberis stenophylla	Barberry	Yellow	3 (10)	3 (10)	E

Cytisus albus	Portugal Broom	White	2·1 (7)	1·8 (6)	E
Cytisus praecox	Broom	Cream	1·5 (5)	1·5 (5)	E
Forsythia suspensa	Golden Bells	Sulphur	2·1 (7)	2·75 (9)	D
Magnolia soulangeana	Magnolia	White, purple	4·25(14)	4·25(14)	D
Osmanthus delavayi	Fragrant Olive	White	1·8 (6)	2·1 (7)	E
Pieris forrestii	Lily of the Valley Shrub	White	1·8 (6)	1·5 (5)	E
Rhododendron augustinii	Rhododendron	Mauve-blue	2·75(9)	2·1 (7)	E
Rhododendron williamsianum	Rhododendron	Pink	·6 (2)	·9 (3)	E
Ribes Scarlet	Flowering Currant	Scarlet	2·5 (8)	1·5 (5)	D
Rosmarinus officinalis	Rosemary	Lavender	1·5 (5)	1·5 (5)	E
Spiraea arguta	Bridal Wreath	White	1·5 (5)	1·5 (5)	D
Ulex europaeus plenus	Double Gorse	Yellow	2·5 (8)	1·8 (6)	E
Viburnum carlesii	Viburnum	Pink, white	1·2 (4)	1·5 (5)	D

May

Azaleas (various)	Azalea	Various	1·2 (4)	1·5 (5)	D&E
Berberis stenophylla	Barberry	Yellow	3 (10)	2·75(9)	E
Ceanothus dentatus	Californian Lilac	Bright blue	3 (10)	3 (10)	E
Choisya ternata	Mexican Orange	White	2·1 (7)	1·8 (6)	E
Cytisus scoparius	Broom	Various	1·8 (6)	1·8 (6)	D
Daphne cneorum	Garland Flower	Rose-pink	·3 (1)	·9 (3)	E
Deutzia elegantissima	Deutzia	Pink	1·25(4½)	1·8 (6)	D
Genista hispanica	Spanish Gorse	Yellow	·6 (2)	1·2 (4)	D
Kerria japonica	Batchelor's Buttons	Yellow	2·5 (8)	1·8 (6)	D
Magnolia liliflora	Magnolia	Red-purple	3·5(12)	3·3(11)	D

Flowering shrubs and month of flowering (continued)

Latin name	Common name	Colour	Height in m(ft)	Spread in m(ft)	
Paeonia suffruticosa	Tree Paeony	Various	1·2 (4)	·9 (3)	D
Rhododendron Hybrids	Rhododendron	Various	2·5 (8)	2·75(9)	E
Spiraea vanhouttei	Spiraea	White	2·5 (8)	2·5 (8)	E
Syringa vulgaris	Lilac	White to purple	3·3(11)	2·75(9)	D
Viburnum opulus sterile	Snowball Tree	White	3 (10)	2·5 (8)	D
Weigela rosea	Weigela	Pink or ruby	1·8 (6)	1·8 (6)	D

June

Buddleia globosa	Orange Ball Tree	Orange	3·3(11)	2·25(9)	SE
Cistus purpureus	Rock Rose	Rosy-crimson	1·5 (5)	1·8 (6)	E
Cornus kousa chinensis	Dogwood	White	2·5 (8)	1·8 (6)	D
Cytisus scoparius	Broom	Various	1·8 (6)	1·8 (6)	D
Daphne Somerset	Daphne	Pale pink	·9 (3)	1·2 (4)	D
Deutzia scabra	Deutzia	White to rose	2·5 (8)	2·5 (8)	D
Genista virgata	Madeira Broom	Yellow	2·75(9)	2·5 (8)	D
Kalmia latifolia	Calico Bush	Shell pink	1·8 (6)	1·8 (6)	E
Philadelphus lemoinei	Mock Orange	White, purple	2·1 (7)	1·8 (6)	D
Phlomis fruticosa	Jerusalem Sage	White, yellow	·9 (3)	1·2 (4)	D
Potentilla fruticosa	Cinquefoil	White, yellow	·6–1·2(2–4)	1·2 (4)	D
Pryacantha coccinea	Firethorn	White	3·5(12)	3·5(12)	E
Senecio laxifolius	Senecio	Yellow	·9 (3)	1·2 (4)	E
Skimmia japonica	Skimmia	White	·9 (3)	1·25(4½)	E

	Spiraea	White	2·5 (8)	2·5 (8)	2·5 (8)	D
Spiraea veitchii						

July

Abutilon vitifolium	Tree Mallow	Mauve	2·1 (7)	1·2 (4)	D
Buddleia davidii	Purple Buddleia	White to purple	2·5 (8)	1·8 (6)	D
Calluna H. E. Beale	Ling – Heather	Rose	·6 (2)	·6 (2)	E
Ceanothus azureus	Californian Lilac	Pink, blue	2·1 (6)	1·5 (5)	D
Hebe brachysiphon	Veronica	White	1·2 (4)	1·2 (4)	E
Hydrangea macrophylla	Hydrangea	White to purple	1·5 (5)	1·8 (6)	D
Hypericum Hidote	St John's Wort	Yellow	1·8 (6)	1·8 (6)	SE
Lavandula officinalis	Lavender	Mauve to purple	·6 (2)	·9 (3)	E
Olearia haastii	Daisy Bush	White	1·5 (5)	1·2 (4)	E
Philadelphus coronarius	Mock Orange	White	2·5 (8)	1·8 (6)	D
Rhus cotinus	Smoke Plant	Purple	2·5 (8)	3 (10)	D
Spartium junceum	Spanish Broom	Yellow	2·5 (8)	2·1 (7)	D
Spiraea Anthony Waterer	Spiraea	Crimson	·9 (3)	1·2 (4)	D

August

Buddleia davidii	Purple Buddleia	White to pink	2·5 (8)	1·8 (6)	D
Ceanothus burkwoodii	Californian Lilac	Bright blue	3 (10)	2·75 (9)	E
Ceratostigma willmottianum	Plumbago	Bright blue	·45 (1½)	·9 (3)	D
Daboecia cantabrica	Irish Heath	Purple	·6 (2)	·9 (3)	E
Erica tetralix	Cross-leaved Heath	White to ruby	·3 (1)	·6 (2)	E

* E = *Evergreen*   SE = *Semi-evergreen*   D = *Deciduous*

Flowering shrubs and month of flowering (continued)

Latin name	Common name	Colour	Height in m(ft)	Spread in m(ft)	
Erica vagans	Cornish Heath	White to cerise	·3 (1)	·6 (2)	E
Fuchsia (hardy kinds)	Fuchsia	Pink to purple	·9 (3)	·9 (3)	D
Hebe hybrids	Veronica	White, pink, blue, purple, crimson	·6 (2)	·9 (3)	E
Hibiscus syriacus	Tree Hollyhock	Blue to crimson	1·8 (6)	1·5 (4)	D
Hydrangea paniculata	Hardy Hydrangea	Cream	1·8 (6)	1·8 (6)	D
Leycesteria formosa	Himalayan Honeysuckle	Claret	2·5 (8)	1·2 (4)	D
Perowskia Blue Spire	Afghan Sage	Deep blue	1·8 (6)	2·1 (7)	D
September					
Caryopteris calandonensis	Blue Spiraea	Bright blue	·9 (3)	1·2 (4)	D
Ceanothus azureus	Californian Lilac	Pink, blue	1·8 (6)	1·8 (6)	D
Erica ciliaris	Dorset Heath	Purple	·3 (1)	·45(1½)	E
Hebe salicifolia	Willow Veronica	White	1·2 (4)	·9 (3)	E
Hibiscus syriacus	Tree Hollyhock	Blue to crimson	1·8 (6)	1·8 (6)	D
Tamarix pentandra	Tamarisk	Rose	2·1 (7)	2·5 (8)	D
October					
Calluna vulgaris	Heather	White to purple	·6 (2)	·9 (3)	E
Ceanothus azureus	Californian Lilac	Pink, blue	1·8 (6)	1·8 (6)	D
Erica vagans	Cornish Heath	White to cerise	·3 (1)	·6 (2)	E

Hebe (hardy kinds)	Veronica	White, pink, blue, purple, crimson	·75(2½)	·9 (3)	E
Leycesteria formosa	Himalayan Honeysuckle	Claret	2·5 (8)	1·2 (4)	E
November					
Erica darleyensis	Heather	Rose-purple	·6 (2)	·45(1½)	E
Hebe (hardy kinds)	Veronica	White, pink, blue, purple, crimson	·6 (2)	·9 (3)	E
Viburnum fragrans	Viburnum	Pale pink	2·75(9)	2·5 (8)	D
December					
Galluna vulgaris	Heather	White to purple	·6 (2)	·9 (3)	E
Erica Winter Beauty	Heather	Deep pink	·3 (1)	·6 (2)	E
Erica darleyensis	Heather	Rose-purple	·6 (2)	·6 (2)	E
Viburnum bobnantense	Viburnum	Deep rose	3 (10)	2·5 (8)	D
Viburnum fragrans	Viburnum	Pale pink	2·75 (9)	2·1 (7)	D

* E = *Evergreen*   SE = *Semi-evergreen*   D = *Deciduous*

Bulb planting table

Plant		Depth in cm(in)	Distance apart cm(in)
Allium	October	10(4)	10(4)
Anemone fulgens	October	7·5(3)	15(6)
Anemone (St Brigid)	October	7·5(3)	15(6)
Anthericum	October	10(4)	15(6)
Antholyza	October	7·5(3)	15(6)
Belladonna Lily	August	22(9)	30(12)
Bluebells	August	5–10(2–4)	7–10(3–4)
Brodiaea	October	10(4)	7·5(3)
Bulbocodium	August	7·5(3)	7·5(3)
Camassia	October	10(4)	10(4)
Chionodoxa	August	7·5(3)	7·5(3)
Colchicum	August	7·5(3)	7·5(3)
Crinum	October	15(6)	45(18)
Crocosmia	Spring	15(6)	10(4)
Crocus	August	7·5(3)	7·5(3)
Daffodils	August	15(6)	15(6)
Erythronium	August	7·5(3)	5(2)
Fritillaria	August	10(4)	10–15(4–6)
Galtonia	November	15(6)	15(6)
Gladiolus	April	10(4)	15(6)
Gladiolus Colvillei type	November	15(6)	15(6)
Hyacinths	October	7–10(3–4)	20(8)
Iris, English	September	7·5(3)	10–15(4–6)
Iris, Spanish	September	7·5(3)	15(6)
Iris reticulata	September	7·5(3)	7·5(3)
Leucojum	August	10(4)	7·5(3)
Lilium auratum	October	15–20(6–8)	15(6)
Lilium Henryi	October	15–20(6–8)	15(6)
Lilium pardalinum	October	10(4)	15(6)
Lilium speciosum	October	15–20(6–8)	15(6)
Lilium tigrinum	October	15(6)	15(6)
Lily of the valley	November	5(2)	5–7·5(2–3)
Montbretia	March	7·5(3)	5(2)
Muscari	October	7·5(3)	7·5(3)
Orange lily (L. croceum)	October	10(4)	15(6)
Ornithogalum	October	10(4)	5–7·5(2–3)
Scilla sibirica	August	7·5(3)	10(4)

Plant		Depth in cm(in)	Distance apart cm(in)
Snowdrop	August	5(2)	2·5(1)
Sternbergia	July	10–15(4–6)	5–7·5(2–3)
Trillium	October	7·5(3)	10(4)
Tritonia	October	10(4)	7–10(3–4)
Tulips, long-stemmed	November	15(6)	22(9)
Tulips, short-stemmed	November	10(4)	15(6)
Winter Aconite	August	5–7·5(2–3)	5(2)

Succession with Brassicas, or members of the 'cabbage' family

Vegetables	Sow	Plant	Distance apart cm(ft)	Varieties	Season
Autumn-heading broccoli	Early April	Early July	60(2)	Veitch's Self-Protecting	Sept/Nov
Mid-winter-heading broccoli	Mid-April	Mid-July	60(2)	Snows Winter White	Dec/March
Spring-heading broccoli	End April	End July	60 (2)	April	April/June
Sprouting broccoli	March	Late June	60(2)	Calabrese	Sept/Nov
Early purple sprouting broccoli	Mid-April	Mid-July	75(2½)	Early Purple Sprouting	Dec./March
Late purple sprouting broccoli	End April	End July	75(2½)	Late Purple Sprouting	April/June
Early Brussels sprouts	Late Jan to Mid-Feb. in frames	Mid-May	75(2½)	Early Dwarf	Oct/Dec
Mid-season Brussels sprouts	March	May/June	90(3)	Exhibition	Nov/Jan
Late Brussels sprouts	Early April	Mid-June	75(2½)	Fasolt New	Dec/April
Spring cabbage	Mid-July	Mid-Sept	38(1½)	Durham Early, Clucas First-Early 218	March/June
Summer cabbage	Mid-Feb	Mid-April	45(1½)	Primo, Wiam	July/Aug
Late summer cabbage	March in frames	Mid-June	45(1½)	Greyhound	Aug/Sept

Autumn cabbage	Mid-April	Mid-July	60(2)	Winninstadt	Sept/Nov
Winter cabbage	End April	End July	60(2)	Christmas-Drumhead, January King	Jan/April
Early summer cauliflower	January in heat	Plant o/s April	45(1½)	Early Snowball	June
Summer cauliflower	Mid-Feb in heat	Mid-April	45(1½)	Snowdrift	June/Aug
Autumn cauliflower	Mid-April	Mid-July	60(2)	Autumn Giant	Sept/Oct
Curled kale	End April	End July	75(2½)	Dwarf Green	Jan/May
Asparagus kale	End April	End July	60(2)	Asparagus	April/May
Cottager's kale	End April	End July	75(2½)	Cottager's	April/June
Labrador kale	Mid-April	Mid-July	60(2)	Labrador	Feb/May
Early Savoy	Mid-April	Mid-July	45(1½)	Best of all	Oct/Dec
Mid Savoy	Mid-April	Mid-July	60(2)	Wisa	Nov/Feb
Late Savoy	End April	End July	60(2)	Ormskirk Extra Late	March/April

Glossary

Access frame Rigid, large-capacity, well-constructed frame with vertical sides which covers plants and ensures quicker growth.

Acid soil Soil which has a pH of 5 or below, ie. a soil which is not limy.

Alkaline soil Soil which has a pH of 9 or above, ie. a soil which is limy.

Bedding Planting out plants from boxes or pots to form a particular pattern in a flower bed.

Blanching A method of keeping out the light so that the green colouring of a stem or leaf is eradicated, leaving the plant white. This can be done by covering a plant out of doors or putting it under the staging of a greenhouse with a curtain in front of it.

Brutting Summer pruning in which the laterals of a plant are broken off with the back of a knife, thus leaving a rough edge. This lets in air and sunlight to the plant, and results in increased fruit production.

Budding Propagating fruit trees or roses by inserting a bud of the desired variety into a suitable stock; usually done in summer.

Chitting tray A shallow tray in which seed potatoes are placed, rose-end upwards, in order to cause the tubers to develop short stubby shoots.

Cordon An apple or pear tree, growing on one stem, trained on wires at 45 degree angles.

Crocks Bits of broken clay pots which are placed in the bottoms of other clay pots to ensure good drainage.

Curd The white central part of the cauliflower.

Deciduous A term applied to trees and shrubs which shed their leaves annually.

Dibbling in Making a hole with a dibber (small stick) for planting cabbages, cauliflowers, etc.

Disbudding Thinning out buds to get fewer and finer flowers.

Family tree Tree which bears a number of different varieties of apples or pears.

Fumigation The vaporization in a greenhouse of special preparations which will produce fumes that will kill insect pests.

Grafting Similar to budding, but instead of a bud a short shoot is used. Outdoor grafting is done in the spring, and indoor grafting is done in the winter in greenhouses.

Hale A storage heap for potatoes and root crops which is often called a clamp.

Haulms The stems and leaves of potatoes.

Hot bed A bed in a frame either heated by decomposing horse manure or by electrical heating wires buried in the soil.

Internode The portion of a stem in between two nodes.

Lorette pruning Pruning back the laterals of plants back to within 3mm($\frac{1}{8}$ in) of their base in the summer.

Mulch A top-dressing of organic matter, such as compost or sedge peat, which is put on the surface of the soil around plants about 2·5 cm (1 in) deep. This helps to retain moisture and deters many pests.

Node The 'joint' of a stem from which a leaf or whorl of leaves emanates.

Pipings Young shoots of plants, usually carnations or pinks, used for propagating.

Reversion A virus disease of blackcurrants when the leaves elongate and no crop is produced.

Ridging The process of digging up stiff heavy clay soil in parallel ridges in the autumn so as to let the frost act on it.

Runner A prostrate shoot which roots at the end, as with strawberries.

Scion The piece of young wood of a particular variety used when grafting on to a stock.

Sedge peat Peat made from sedges and rushes which can be used as a mulch. This kind is much more valuable to plants than sphagnum peat which is made from mosses.

Stooling A method of propagation in which fruit stocks are cut down almost to the ground. This 'stool' then develops many shoots which are earthed up, root, severed from the parent plants and then planted themselves.

Stock The root part of fruit trees which controls the size to which the trees will grow and the age at which the tree will stop growing.

Stopping The pinching out of the growing point of a tomato plant to prevent it from growing any taller.

Striking cuttings When cuttings have produced roots.

Sucker Growth that develops from the roots of some plants.

Wind rocking death The plant rocks back and forth in winter winds, causing a cone-shaped depression to be formed at its base. Water collects in this and the plant is killed.

Index